The
Great
Themes

The Great Themes

WORLD MYTH

MYTH AND MANKIND

THE GREAT THEMES: World Myth
Writers: Tony Allan (The Meaning of Myth, A World Alive With Gods
and Spirits, God-Kings and Supermen, Confronting the Final Mystery,
An Enduring Legacy), Charles Phillips (In the Beginning)

Created, edited and designed by
Duncan Baird Publishers
Castle House
75–76 Wells Street
London W1P 3RE

DUNCAN BAIRD PUBLISHERS
Managing Editor: Diana Loxley
Managing Art Editor: Clare Thorpe
Series Editor: Christopher Westhorp
Editor: Christopher Westhorp
Designer: Christine Keilty
Picture Researchers: Cecilia Weston-Baker, Christine Keilty, Emily Stone
Commissioned Illustrations: Neil Gower
Artwork Borders: Iona McGlashan

TIME-LIFE BOOKS
Time-Life INC. President and CEO: George Artandi
Time-Life International President: Stephen R. Frary

Staff for THE GREAT THEMES: World Myth
Editorial Manager: Tony Allan
Design Consultant: Mary Staples
Editorial Production: Alexia Turner

Published by Time-Life Books BV, Amsterdam
First Time-Life English language printing 2000
TIME-LIFE is a trademark of
Time Warner Inc, USA

ISBN 0 7054 3683 7

Colour separation by Colourscan, Singapore
Printed and bound by Milanostampa, SpA, Farigliano, Italy

Title page: The enigmatic face of the Egyptian goddess Hathor stares
from a column capital at Dendara, her cult centre dating from Old
Kingdom times. Daughter of the sun god, she was associated with a
wide variety of things, including motherly nurturing, beauty and love,
music and revelry, and welcoming souls to the afterlife.

Contents page: Totem pole carving of the legendary Thunderbird
from whose eyes flashed lightning and whose wings beat thunder.
The human face reflected a local belief that animals possessed human
souls. Haida people of North America's Northwest Coast culture.

30 29 28 27 26 25 24 23 22 21 20 19 18 17 16 15 14 13 12 11 10 9 8 7 6 5 4 3 2 1

Contents

THE MEANING OF MYTH

Myths are magic mirrors in which we can see the reflection of not just our own hopes and fears but also those of people from the earliest times. For some of the stories are unimaginably old; almost certainly people were recounting them long before the birth of writing and the dawn of recorded history. Collectively they represent the world's heritage of the imagination. They lie at the roots of much of its literature, philosophy and religion.

For the people who originally told them, the myths served many purposes. They provided answers to the great philosophical questions – how the universe came into being, the nature of the forces operating within it, the origins of the first people and of the human community. And they also addressed more intimate issues, providing guidance on personal behaviour, social rules and what might happen to those who died. Collectively, they provided the mental foundations of understanding and belief on which individuals could build their lives. And, crucially, they did so in narrative form. They told stories that people could remember and identify with, that could make them laugh, feel awe and cry.

Because the questions they address are so large, myths have always had an interest that crosses cultural boundaries. Yet anyone studying the subject quickly makes a surprising discovery. It is impossible to spend any length of time comparing the world's myths without being struck by the odd resemblances that link them. The same images – an egg from which the cosmos hatched; a universal flood; a perilous bridge to the land of the dead – crop up again and again.

The similarities are sufficiently marked to have attracted the attention of scholars from many intellectual disciplines who, over the years in their respective fields, have sought an explanation for them. One obvious line of enquiry lay in cultural diffusion – the idea that myths travelled from people to people through direct contact, just as trade goods might have done. This suggestion at one time seemed to go far to explain the mystery. In the nineteenth century, for example, much was made of the spread of the Indo-European languages across Eurasia in the Bronze Age. One branch of the Aryan peoples credited with transmitting the tongues went to India, while another passed through the Middle East and Greece to northern Europe. Here was an obvious route of transmission that could explain how some common themes appear in both Indian, Greek and Norse mythology.

The picture became more complicated in the twentieth century as Westerners learned more about the myths of Australasia, sub-Saharan Africa and the Americas – places that had no physical links in early times with the joint Eurasian myth stock. Yet their stories too shared some of the same common features. It turned out that there were deluge myths from Australia and South America just as there were from China and Mesopotamia, and creation stories from Africa that paralleled those from ancient Greece. Some other factor seemed to be at work, bridging distances that past populations had never spanned.

The problem caught the attention of the great Swiss psychiatrist Carl Gustav Jung, a friend and colleague of Sigmund Freud. Jung further noted that many of the symbols that recur repeatedly in world myth – dark forests, abrupt transformations, monstrous creatures, abandoned children, descriptions of flying or falling – also featured in his own dreams and those of his patients. He used this connection to formulate his theory of the collective unconscious – a section of the unconscious mind made up of memories and images shared with all humankind. Although many people have since challenged his view that this awareness is inborn, the attendant notion of archetypes – the term he used to describe universally recognized mental symbols – has passed into common currency.

Above: Japanese myth was filled with heroic warrior exploits and the all-pervasive *kami* of the natural world. Woodblock print of a water spirit by Kunimasa, 19th century.

Left: Twins were feared and welcomed in equal measure, often providing symbols of contradiction and unity. Luba stool, Congo, 19th century.

Below: Bronze ritual wine vessel of China's Middle Western Zhou period, 10th century BC. Such items offered proof of the owner's status to the deceased ancestors who were believed to drink from it.

These archetypes, in Jung's view, were the missing link between the individual mind and myth. And it is they that make the great themes underlying world mythology relevant to this day. "That's a myth," people say, implying something is ridiculous or untrue; but they also speak of something that touches them profoundly as having "a mythic dimension".

And that is why individuals still look to the old tales to help make sense of their own lives and the world around them. The fact is that the great themes of myth parallel our own experience. They play out on an imaginative plane our deepest hopes and fears.

And they carry a social message, too. They suggest that underneath the huge differences of language and outlook that separate the world's cultures, there may be a common foundation. Something still not fully explained in the structure of the human mind may cause peoples of all continents and climes to thrill to the same plotlines and respond to the same dramas. . In this respect, myths are signposts to the world before Babel, brought together again by the common language of story. Recurring with endless variation from culture to culture, they demonstrate timelessly the essential imaginative unity of the human race.

IN THE BEGINNING

Billions of years ago, according to scientists, the universe was concentrated in a single, unimaginably dense point that exploded in a "Big Bang" – and matter has been moving apart ever since. One day, the resulting energy will run down and the universe will die. In setting the boundaries of our existence, science helps shape our consciousness, our sense of who we are. In previous eras myths filled the same need, providing answers to the troubling questions "Where from?", "How?" and "Why?"

A myth explaining the beginnings of the universe is known as a cosmogony – from the Greek *kosmos* ("order") and *genesis* ("birth"). Such tales describe how things came to be ordered and comprehensible: they usually imagine a time before order, when all was *chaos* ("void"), and describe how order emerged or was brought forth. In doing so, the myths generally served to sustain the status quo, the existing power structures of the culture from which they emerged. Ancient Egyptian and Mesopotamian cosmogonic myths survived in different versions promoting the importance of regional and city gods; Aztec myths reinforced priestly prestige and the hold of sacrifice rituals. Such tales made clear both how things came to be arranged as they were and also – equally importantly – why they should continue in the same way.

In some cultures cosmogonic myths also served to sustain a people's way of life, passing on information about landscape and survival skills. Native American myths, for example, explained to their audience not only where the tribe came from – often a dark underworld – but also in some detail how the land took its present form and why certain animals could be found in particular places and behaved in certain ways. For Australian Aborigines, the Dreamtime was not a distant past event but a dimension that resonated in the landscape, and tribal mythology – through their "song lines" and "dreaming tracks" – provided guidance for survival in the desert.

For all peoples, cosmogonies marked out the limits of life on Earth – many envisaged how the world would end as well as how it had begun – and also explained how and why people came to be here. Persian Zoroastrianism taught that humankind was created to struggle against evil in the cosmos – and one day all would be cleansed of it and gathered before the Wise Lord, Ahura Mazda. Such myths of beginning and end gave peoples purpose and meaning in their lives.

Opposite: Modern science enables us to view and explore the vastness of the universe, as well as to appreciate how much more the ancients understood than was once believed. Our galaxy, the Milky Way, contains 100 billion stars and is seen here in the constellation of Scorpio, photographed from Arizona, USA.

Below: The world as an egg was one of the more widespread cosmological notions. This rock depicts the "bird man" of Easter Island holding the egg associated with the creator, Makemake.

Order Out of Chaos

In the beginning, many myths tell us, order replaced chaos. Either this occurred spontaneously, or because a creator divinity willed it. Cultural interpretations varied, but generally formlessness was given shape and unity gave way to multiplicity and variety.

What came before the order of the existing universe was terrifying and essentially unknowable – formless and endless, without boundaries or depths. The imagery used to describe this state recurred across cultures: a cloud, a vast wasteland, or a shifting mass of water, swathed in darkness.

The Mesopotamian creation story *Enuma Elish* ("When on high. . .") dates from at least the twelfth century BC and may be a good deal older. In its account, before Heaven and Earth there was only water – either salt or fresh, personified respectively as the god Apsu and the goddess Tiamat. They were together, commingled, and from them the first gods and the universe came into being. The image of chaos as lapping waters was almost certainly widespread in the ancient Middle East, and many writers have noted its similarity to the picture given in the Biblical account of God moving through darkness across the waters.

One story told by Polynesian islanders also contained this image of chaos as a shifting ocean – and bore a striking resemblance to the Biblical version. It revealed that once there was only an endless ocean bathed in darkness and inhabited by

the creator Io. He spoke and made light, then after a while spoke once more to bring back darkness: the first day and night.

In some accounts, life began in the void on its own, without divine intervention. According to Tibet's native Bon religion, primeval chaos was a void that spontaneously brought forth matter. In the Japanese tradition, too, the cosmos generated itself from chaos, taking form as the High Plain of Heaven and the initially shapeless Earth far below.

Northern European Norse myth told how life was born in a desolate void or abyss called Ginnungagap from a chance interaction of melting ice and fire. This place of nothingness lay between a land of flames named Muspell to the south and a barren, freezing land named Niflheim to the north; in Niflheim eleven rivers rose and deposited lees that froze to ice, covering the void. Muspell's heat melted some of that ice, and life began in those waters. This grim image was most likely inspired by the volcanic northern landscape familiar to the tellers of Icelandic myths, suggesting their early influence on Viking and Germanic stories. In other accounts, Niflheim was held to be the land of the dead and existed on a lower level, beneath the land of mortals (see pages 18–21).

The Universal Cosmic Egg

In the majority of accounts, however, a mysterious process accounted for the divine creator's birth. One early Greek myth attributed creation to a goddess who came to life in the void of chaos. Emerging from nothingness, she created the waters and danced upon them. Her motions caused a wind to spring up, and she used this material to

Many creation stories told of the desolation of the first places. These giant rocks dominate a forbidding landscape in a region of western Ireland called The Burren.

make a companion for herself: a vast snake. She was embraced by the snake, then turned into a dove and laid an egg. From the egg came all life. Later, when the snake became proud, she banished it to the underworld. Later still, she created the first man.

The Greek vision included many images that recurred across cultures, and the vast egg that contained the potentiality of life was a widespread image for the void itself. (Some writers have even suggested that this "cosmic egg" has a modern counterpart in the primeval fireball of the Big Bang theory. The fireball, like the egg, contained the entire universe in potential form.)

It is easy to understand why an egg should have been associated with the beginning of life: by everyday observation early peoples could see that

new life came from eggs laid by birds or snakes. Such creation myths are found in Indian, Chinese, Tibetan and Japanese traditions, and it has been speculated that these may all have had a common source. The cosmic egg is also found in ancient Egyptian mythology, as well as in more southerly parts of Africa, in some Polynesian myths and in Finland, as told in the *Kalevala*, a nineteenth-century epic derived from folklore (see box below).

In China's best-known creation myth, primeval chaos was a cloud of moisture in the shape of an egg. The creator, Pan Gu, took the form of a sturdy man, and he awoke to life at the heart of the egg. His movements broke the egg open, spilling the elements of life far and wide: the purer ones floated upwards to become Heaven and the heavier ones sank to become the Earth.

Ilmatar and the Seven Eggs

Creation from a cosmic egg that contained all future life within it, together with the appearance of a primeval bird that fluttered over the first waters, were two concepts found worldwide that were also familiar to the Finns of northern Europe.

Both elements feature in the Finnish epic poem, the *Kalevala*, created by the writer Elias Lonnrot in the nineteenth century from fragments of folkloric poems.

Before the universe came into being there were only restless waters beneath endless sky. Ilmatar, the daughter of the sky, descended to the waters and swam there for 700 years, always longing for companionship – for new life to share the wild spaces. Then along came a teal, a small duck, seeking a place to build her nest. Ilmatar raised one floating knee to make a dry space. On this first island, the

bird laid six eggs of gold and one of iron.

The teal dutifully incubated her eggs, creating such heat that Ilmatar's knee began to burn. When the goddess could stand it no more she moved the knee, spilling the eggs into the waters and creating strong winds and heaving waves.

This storm broke the eggs open, and from one of them the sun, the moon, land and all the stars of the heavens emerged. Many centuries later, Ilmatar created the natural features of the world, and the animals and fish with which it throngs.

This division was explained in terms of the traditional Chinese distinction between the female passive quality of yin (the heavy Earth) and the male active quality of yang (the purer heavens). Japanese mythology also posited an egg whose elements separated, and the same image – sometimes derived from light or moisture – appeared in many Tibetan myths too; in one account, the void of chaos gave forth a blue radiance, which became a rainbow, then steam, then lightly falling dew, finally becoming a magnificent egg that gave issue to the universe.

According to one of many complex creation myths told by the Dogon people of Mali in western Africa, the creator god Amma himself took the form of a great egg. Like the other cosmic eggs, he contained within his oval shape the potential for all life. The enclosed elements eventually came together in an explosion that started creation.

This Chinese mother-of-pearl disc – a shape used to represent the sky – has at its centre the symbols of yin and yang, the opposing but complementary energy-forms at the heart of all existence. These forces were unleashed from the primal egg by Pan Gu.

The Power of the Divine Mind

In another Dogon myth, Amma designed the universe mentally, then wrote on the void, using signs of water that took material form. The emergence of order from nothingness by the mental power of the creator is a central theme in Indian mythology too. The early mythological understanding alluded to in the *Rig Veda* scripture was that the creator was Mind, consciousness and self-awareness that emerged from the void. In a celebrated later myth, the entire universe existed within the meditation of Brahma, the creator; the heavens, the world and all its peoples were the thoughts of the god. According to this version, the deity Vishnu – worshipped as the preserver of all things – came into existence out of nothing,

created the endless primordial waters and reclined upon the 100-headed serpent Ananta-Shesha, who represented eternity. As Vishnu rested, a lotus arose from his navel and it opened to reveal Brahma, who produced and maintained the universe by the power of his thoughts. This creation occurs repeatedly within a vast recurring cycle (see page 39).

In another major Indian account, the divine consciousness that sustains all things emerged from the void and created the primordial waters. It loosed a seed into the waters that became a great golden egg that glowed mysteriously with all the power of the sun. Meditating within was the god Brahma, who used the spiritual energy or *tapas* generated by his mental activity to break open the cosmic egg. He then used its elements to create the universe.

Life-giving Waters

The central creation myth of the ancient Egyptians maintained that the beginnings of life came with the emergence of a mound of fertile land from Nun, the waters of chaos. The Egyptians' understanding was shaped, like that of the Norse, by the conditions of their own life: the annual flooding of the Nile left behind rich layers of silt that fed the crops. In one version, told in Hermopolis in central Egypt, eight deities – the Ogdoad (Group of Eight) – came to life in the waters of chaos. They were four male frogs and four female snakes. When they came together, the fertile mound emerged. On it was a golden egg that split; the mound turned to flame and the great sun god Re rose into the skies. In another account, the god Amun in the form of a serpent or a goose existed first and created the Ogdoad; in another the cosmic egg was laid on the mound by a heron.

13

The Birth of the Gods

In most traditions, the emergence of order from chaos was not followed at once by the appearance of men and women. One or, more commonly, several generations of deities, often personifications of physical features, first materialized in the newly formed cosmos.

In the tales of the Mixtec of Mexico, the first divinity was a culture hero called Lord Nine Wind, who lifted the sky – which, in common with many other American peoples, they believed was made of water – away from the Earth. In the wake of his act two divinities emerged from the mist that covered the new Earth – a god named One Deer "Lion Serpent" and a beautiful goddess called One Deer "Jaguar Serpent". These two were essentially one: male and female aspects of a single deity. From their interaction the gods of the Mixtec pantheon were born. Similarly, the supreme god of the nearby Aztecs was both two and one: Ometeotl – "Lord of Duality" – had two identities, one male, one female, which together sustained the universe.

According to the ancient Greek poet Hesiod's *Theogeny*, written in the eighth century BC, the first goddesses and gods emerged from the void of chaos and then gave issue to further generations of deities. Five emerged from chaos: they were Gaia (Earth), Tartarus (Underworld), Eros (Sexual Desire), Nyx (Night) and Erebus (the darkness of the underworld). Without any form of sexual congress, Gaia produced children – Uranus, the tall

The sun god Re once reigned over the universe he had created, watching over his kingdom through an all-seeing, removable eye. Here, a falcon-headed Re is shown during his journey across the heavens on the Barque of Millions of Years, c.990BC. Re was also identified with other powerful gods such as Amun and Atum.

Izanagi and Izanami were the seventh male-female pair of gods to be created but their predecessors played little part in Japan's tales of creation. Izanagi and Izanami performed the role of Adam and Eve in the Shinto pantheon. The primal couple, they formed the islands of Japan from the primeval ocean, married and begat all the life-forms found in the natural world – but through their subsequent actions they introduced mortality too.

star-kissed sky; Pontus, the sea; and the towering mountains. Nyx mated with Erebus, bringing forth, among others, Day. Gaia then lay with Uranus and gave birth to many more children – including the Titans, the first rulers of the universe, who were subsequently overthrown by Gaia's grandson Zeus.

Of Sky and Earth

In other traditions the creator god, having produced order from chaos, proceeded to give issue to a generation of self-propagating gods. Ometeotl, through Tonacatecuhtli ("Lord of our Sustenance") and Tonacacihuatl ("Lady of our Sustenance"), his male and female identities, gave issue to four sons, representative of the four quarters of the Earth. These sons – Red Tezcatlipoca (Xipe Totec), Black Tezcatlipoca (later simply Tezcatlipoca), White Tezcatlipoca (Quetzalcoatl) and Blue Tezcatlipoca (Huitzilopochtli) – were, like their parents, in truth aspects of a single god, their grandfather.

In Maori creation lore, Io, the ultimate creator, gave issue to the earth goddess Papa and the sky god Rangi. From their union the other gods came forth. A similar understanding informs the birth of the first gods and goddesses described in the Mesopotamian *Enuma Elish*. From the complementary male-female water deities Apsu and Tiamat were born Lahmu and Lahamu, who in turn came together and produced Anshar and Kishar, representatives of the horizon between Earth and sky. Anshar's offspring were the tall heavens.

According to one ancient Egyptian account, the god Atum – one manifestation of the sun-creator god, who was self-generating and materialized on the fertile mound (see page 13) – spilled his own seed to give issue to twin deities Shu (Air) and Tefnut (Moisture). These gods then coupled, creating divine descendants. Shu and Tefnut gave issue to Geb (Earth) and Nut (Sky). Geb and Nut lay together – like Gaia and Uranus – and produced more divinities, including Osiris, god of order, and Seth, god of disorder.

The generative power of the union of sky and earth was clear for early peoples to see: from the sky came the life-giving rain that fed rivers, plants and the first farmed crops. In the Greek context, the opposition between sky and earth divinities had an additional resonance, reflecting the separate traditions of the native Greeks, a people who worshipped a fertility mother goddess linked to the earth, and the Indo-European Aryan nomads

15

Messengers of the Deities

In many mythical and religious traditions the gods rely on the help of messengers – an assortment of go-betweens who descend to the human world in order to do the divine beings' bidding.

The Norse told of the Valkyries, mounted maidens with golden hair and dazzling white skin who appeared over human battlefields. They did the will of Odin, chief of the gods, and conducted worthy warriors across the rainbow bridge to their reward in Valhalla, the feasting hall of fallen heroes that lay in Asgard, land of the gods.

It was often one of the messengers' principal tasks to lead the dead to the afterlife. In ancient Greek tradition, Zeus's messenger Hermes was the only one of the Olympian gods to have access to all three worlds – the gods' abode on Mount Olympus, the world of humans and the underworld of the dead. Both Hermes and his Roman counterpart Mercury conducted souls to the underworld.

Hermes's name came from the *herma*, rockpiles used to identify frontiers and roads: as well as the gods' messenger he was a god of boundaries and a trickster associated with sexual licence, gambling, mischief and thievery. In this he matched the West African tricksters Legba, revered by the Fon of Dahomey (modern Benin), and Eshu, honoured by the neighbouring Yoruba. Both Eshu and Legba were interpreters and go-betweens for the gods.

They also controlled divination and magic – as did the ancient Egyptians' divine messenger, the moon god Thoth, who was said to have written the first book of magic spells.

Within the Judaeo-Christian and Islamic traditions, angels were seen as messengers, mingling with mortals, bringing warnings and messages from on high. Some scholars have speculated that in monotheistic religions angels were a survival of the ancient animistic goddesses and gods who had been worshipped by pagan converts. This was demonstrably the case in the ancient Persian

---

who settled much of Greece around 2000BC and whose cult centred on a sky god. When Zeus established his supremacy over Gaia, myth validated the incomers' imposition of their ways on the indigenous peoples they encountered.

Strange Births and Family Roots

The origin of the first Norse gods was quite strange. When the melting ice in the Ginnungagap abyss gave issue to the first life (see page 11), it took the form of Ymir, a giant and father of a race of frost-giants, and a cow named Audhumla. The cow licked at the salty ice and uncovered a huge figure in the form of a man. He was Buri, grandfather of the Norse gods Odin, Vili and Ve.

In Japan's indigenous Shinto religion there are gods and goddesses almost without number, for even individual rocks and trees are believed to have their own *kami* or divine spirits – just as the

ancient Romans also once had their *numina* or *genii loci* (see page 46). The first *kami* emerged in curious fashion. After Earth and the High Plain of Heaven had sprung spontaneously from the egg-shaped cloud of chaos (see page 11), the first three *kami* emerged from a white cloud that floated above the High Plain of Heaven. Below, the Earth had not taken solid form, but it gave issue to a tall reed shoot that climbed to Heaven and became two more *kami*. These deities gave issue to several generations of divinities, and the seventh generation were Izanami and Izanagi, creators of Japan.

The goddess Izanami and the god Izanagi were not only husband and wife but also brother and sister. In many other traditions too, the first generations of gods engaged in incestuous unions, as father lay with daughter, son with mother, brother with sister. Violation of such a deep and widespread social taboo set the gods apart from mere mortals – and may have been intended to

religion of Zoroastrianism, which had a great influence on Judaism, Islam and Christianity. Its angel-like *yazatas* ("Worshipful Ones") such as Mithra, *yazata* of loyalty, and Apam Napat, *yazata* of oaths, had clear links with the pagan divinities of preceding tradition. Angels, too, were linked with magic. In Islam two fallen angels, Harut and Marut, taught mortals the magic arts.

In many cultures, particularly the Arctic and South America, the intermediary between divine and human realms was the shaman, the folk-priest who visited the gods during spirit flights and trances.

Valkyries accompany Odin and Thor in *The Wild Hunt of Odin* by Peter Nicolai Arbo.

validate the practice of incest in royal households (see box, page 83). Mesopotamia's deity Enki, god of fresh water, slept with his daughter, his grand-daughter and his great-granddaughter and gave issue to great gods and goddesses. When the Hindu creator Brahma looked passionately upon Sarasvati, the daughter he had created from his own energy, she was so ashamed because he was her father that she skipped in all four directions away from him, and he grew four heads to follow her with his passionate gaze. Eventually he lay with her, and the fruits of their union were the first man and woman.

Acts of patricide or matricide were also common among the first generations of gods. In Greek myth, Gaia's son Cronos castrated and dethroned his father Uranus. Installed as the new deity of the heavens, Cronos then repeated the union of sky god and earth goddess by marrying his sister Rhea. He in turn was dethroned by his son Zeus.

In Indian tradition the storm god Indra, also born of a union between sky god (Dyaus) and earth goddess (Prithivi), overpowered his father Dyaus and flung him down to his death. Similarly in Mesopotamian tradition the god Marduk killed his great-great-great-grandmother, the creator goddess Tiamat, to become the world's first king.

In the wake of Freud's work, many modern readers might recognize that such episodes drama-tize the powerful feelings of competition that can arise between generations, especially between sons and fathers. Divine patricides also often reflected competition and conflict between the gods of different social groups. Dyaus, for instance, was identified with Varuna, who had once been revered as king of the gods and was the deity of the *brahmin* or priestly class. Indra's triumph over Varuna may thus reflect the prece-dence of the *kshatriyas* (warrior class) over the *brahmins* in the mid-first millennium BC.

17

The Shape of the Universe

Natural curiosity drove early peoples to wonder what lay beyond the lands they knew. In picturing the larger universe, most mythologies imagined a splendid, paradisiacal home for the gods and a separate land for the dead.

Many early peoples believed that divine spirits were all about them, moving, usually invisibly, through the human world, or inhabiting local features such as mountains or lakes. But in their myths they also created a separate home for the most important divinities. The Japanese, for instance, believed that *kami* or deities inhabited the landscape, but also spoke of sky *kami* living in a heavenly realm. According to their schema, the home of the sky *kami* was on the High Plain of Heaven. It was linked by the rainbow, the Floating Bridge of Heaven, to the realm of mortals, the Central Land of the Reed Plain. Beneath the plain was Yomi, the shadowy land of the dead, connected to the islands of Japan either by a winding road that led down into the ground or a deep hole on a lonely, windswept beach.

The familiar picture of Heaven above and an underworld below is found in the pagan religion of ancient Persia and in the influential faith of Zoroastrianism that grew from it – where the Wise Lord Ahura Mazda lived on high surrounded by light and the evil one Angra Mainyu lived beneath, writhing in darkness. This basic image recurs in many Indo-European cultures and elsewhere in Asia, Oceania and the Americas.

A Complex, Layered Universe

Many mythologies developed complex cosmologies with several layers. In Hindu tradition, the world consisted of seven circular lands; the central one was surrounded by a salt sea and supported the sacred peak, Mount Meru. Beneath lay seven vertically stacked layers of Hell, inhabited by serpents and demons, while above climbed seven resplendent layers of Heaven. At the top of Heaven was *brahman*, the home of perfect souls who had escaped the cycle of death and rebirth. Buddhist traditions also recognized Mount Meru; they said it stood above 136 layers of Hell and was surmounted by forty-five Heavens.

The Mesoamerican Maya and Aztec peoples spoke of thirteen layers of Heaven above the Earth and nine layers of underworld beneath. According to the Aztecs, the highest level of Heaven was Omeyocan, home to the creator Ometeotl, and all the levels converged at Tenochtitlan, their capital city. Norse tradition, like that of the Japanese, spoke of three levels – above, Asgard, home of the gods and site of Valhalla; in the middle, Midgard, the realm of humans, and Jotunheim, rocky territory of the giants; and beneath, Niflheim, abode of the dead who were not called to Valhalla. All three levels were linked and supported by Yggdrasill, the World Tree (see box, pages 20–21).

Realms of the Familiar

Certain Siberian peoples believed in thirteen realms, in appearance much like the Earth, inhabited by spirits and accessible to shamans on soul flights. This less formal conception did not propose that the zones were all stacked vertically in

Enlightenment enabled Jain monks to discover the nature of the universe – a cosmos they named *loka* – and they devoted much time and effort to understanding it. This reverent image shows the *loka* as a complex, multi-layered disc of concentric continents and oceans. At the centre is Jambudvipa, the inner continent of the mortal world, divided into seven regions with sacred Mount Meru at its core. Outside Jambudvipa are two other continents and two salt oceans filled with assorted human and animal life.

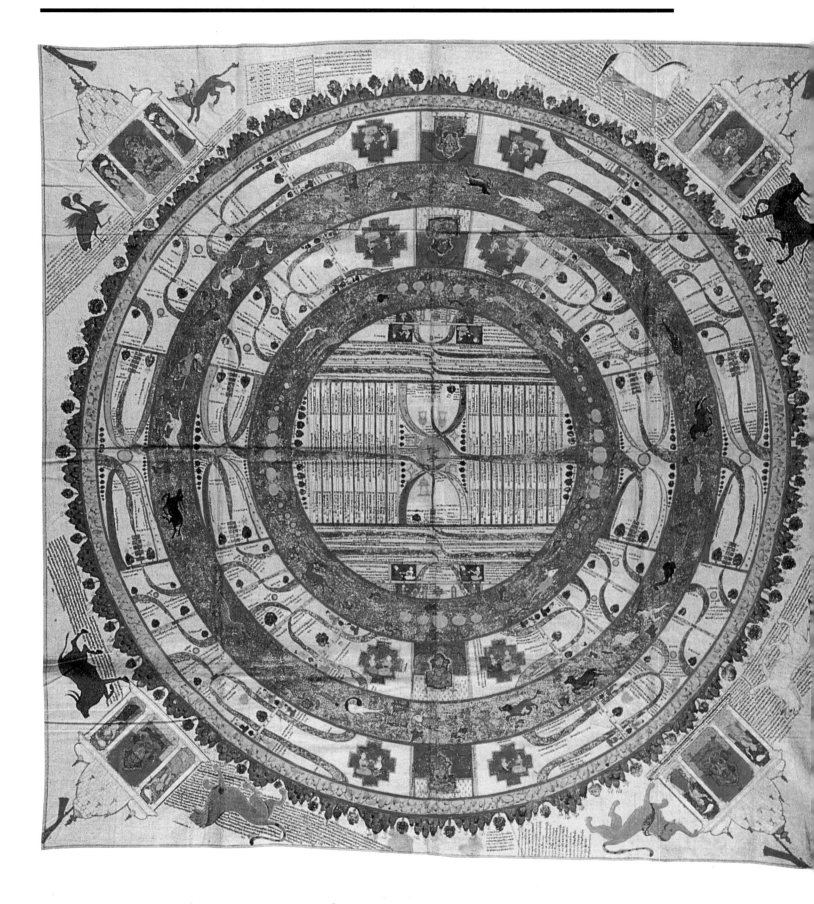

A detail from the 16th-century *Madrid Codex* shows the fourfold nature of the Maya cosmos. The dots radiating from the corners of the central square are days from the ritual calendar, each side marked by pairs of deities and a glyph for geographical direction. To the Maya, the multilayered world was square and oriented to the cardinal directions from a central axis. The cosmos and Maya mythology were intertwined, for the tales were believed to be played out nightly in the movements of stars.

orderly fashion. Instead the realms, while beyond this world, were associated with particular locations within it such as the seabed or sky.

Some peoples placed the home of the gods within the landscape they knew. The ancient Greeks chose an actual peak, Mount Olympus, an isolated mountain rising to almost 3,000 metres that served as a strategically important defence against incomers and raiders from the north. While the real-life mountain was barren and rocky, the Olympus inhabited by Zeus and his extended family of deities was a delightful realm beyond an entranceway of clouds and centred on the magnificent palace of the divine ruler himself. Although the Greeks focused their devotions on the actual Olympus, it was tacitly understood that the gods' true abode was in a realm "beyond" the Earth on which they trod.

In other traditions too, the gods' mythological realm was loosely identified by worshippers with local geography. The Hindus' Mount Meru, for instance, was said to be one of the towering peaks

The Symbolic Importance of Trees

Many myths spoke of a tree of life or a great World Tree supporting the different realms within the universe. In Hindu tradition the entire cosmos was sometimes said to be a vast inverted tree, Asvattha, with its roots spreading out among the heavens and its branches across the Earth.

Some scholars suggest that this downwards movement may have been intended to represent the life-giving descent of the sun's rays. Judaism's Kaballah tradition also spoke of a mystically apprehended Tree of Life.

Shamans from diverse cultures in Mongolia, Slavic eastern Europe and the Americas reported having witnessed in their soul flights a World Tree linking the deep underworld, the encompassing Earth and overarching heavens. The Maya of Central America, peoples of the Sahara region of North Africa and inhabitants of Borneo also described a similar image. For some South American Indians – for instance the Guarani and the Shipibo – the tree's function was to keep the separate realms of sky and Earth apart.

Probably the most celebrated World Tree was the great ash, Yggdrasill, of Norse tradition. It linked the three realms of the universe: one of its roots grew in the underworld, and beneath it was a spring from which came the rivers that led to the creation of all things. Another root grew in the land of the giants in the middle realm and beneath that one was the well of wisdom. The third

THE SHAPE OF THE UNIVERSE

of the Himalayas (see box, page 23). One of the four Heavens revered by the followers of Tibet's Bon religion was Wolmo Lungring, which was vaguely situated in the real world to the west of Tibet – although at the same time it was said to occupy a third of the Earth's surface.

Some peoples likened the shape of the universe to that of a familiar object. To the Fon of West Africa it was akin to a round calabash that had been sliced horizontally in two – the top half held the heavens, while the bottom half was filled with water, in which the Earth floated. For the Polynesian islanders of Nauru, the universe was a clamshell, with the islands floating in the sea in the bottom half and the sky in the top.

In some Chinese accounts, the heavens resembled an overturned bowl, supported by five sacred mountains and covering the square Earth – the whole resembling a Chinese chariot, which had a circular umbrella above a square carriage. Another Chinese account compared the universe to a vast egg, with the heavens spread out across the inner part of the upper shell and the Earth floating in the waters that filled the bottom part.

sprouted in Asgard, land of the gods, by the well of Urd (fate) where the gods held their daily council. At the end of the world, the tree would be the source of new creation (see page 39).

Scholars note that in many disparate traditions the tree was a symbol of wholeness and life, and from it came good things: the Norse god Odin made a voluntary sacrifice of himself and hung in terrible pain upon Yggdrasill in order to gain power over the runes that delivered knowledge.

This 15th-century Veda Druma is a representation of the archetypal Hindu tree of life and knowledge. The tree also symbolizes the human nervous system, which itself holds the key to life's secrets. The central snake sits on a lotus, a feminine symbol of creativity associated with the body's *chakras* or energy centres, for life-energy is said to be expressed through the five senses.

21

Making the Earth

The theory of evolution tells us that life began in the seas, and early peoples also understood the generative power of water: they saw rain nourish their crops and knew that silt left by flooding provided fertile land for sowing. In ancient Egypt life was imagined arising from an earth mound, while others believed that the land itself had emerged from the ocean.

One common explanation is known to scholars as the "earthdiver" myth. A bird or other creature dived to the bottom of the primordial ocean and fetched up mud or sand; when this was scattered on the waters, an expanse of land magically grew. Variations on this theme were widespread among Native Americans. The diver had various identities: the Cherokee of the east said it was a water beetle, their near neighbours the Chickasaw that it was a crayfish; elsewhere it was a beaver, muskrat, mink or duck (see box, pages 24–25). In many accounts the land, when it was made, lay spread upon the back of a great turtle (see page 30).

Curiously, a Christian version of the earthdiver myth is found in central Europe. In this telling, at the beginning of all things there was the great primordial ocean, God and the Devil; God sent the Devil diving to fetch up mud. He succeeded after several attempts, and then God used it to fashion the land. The Devil's involvement and his touch upon the raw materials of creation explain why the universe is flawed and stained with evil.

On the other side of the world, similar myths told how the first land came from sand or earth sprinkled on the ocean – but these raw materials came down from Heaven rather than up from the ocean floor. A Mongolian Buddhist myth featured the Lord Buddha himself, here called Sagjamuni, in the creation, and told how, at a time when there was nothing but water, Sagjamuni threw down from on high a lump of yellow earth that had been given him by the Qormusta, king of the gods. The earth spread to form the continents of the world.

The Yoruba of West Africa recounted how the sky god Olodumare sent down two of his sons from Heaven into the endless sea that was the universe. One of the sons, Oduduwa, opened a bag his father had given him, found some earth and scattered it on the waters to make the first land. Similarly, in Sumatra a creation myth told how the daughter of one of the gods fell from Heaven to the endless primordial waters to escape the unwelcome attentions of another deity. When her father Batara Guru learned of her exile he sent a swallow down with a handful of soil to scatter on the waters and so make the first land.

In Japanese myth the Earth at first floated like oil on the sea's surface and coagulated only when the god Izanagi leaned down from the heavenly rainbow bridge (see page 18) and stirred the water with a spear. For the Hawaiians, whose entire world was islands, the opposite occurred; goddess Pele made the archipelago when she released waters across what had been a great mass of land that she had found in mid-ocean, until finally only the mountain-tops were visible as separate islands.

From a Giant Body

The notion that the Earth is sacred, alive and possessed by spirit was central to pre-Buddhist Tibetan belief. There are many tales describing how particular regions were formed from the bodies of sacred animals, and in one tradition the body of a great *klu* (water spirit) demoness was transformed into the universe: the Earth from her flesh, the sky from her head, the sun and moon from her eyes, the seas from her blood.

The idea that land derived from the body of a vast primeval being was widespread, found in Asia, Polynesia, northern Europe, the Middle East and Central America.

The Sacredness of Earth's Highest Places

If the divine resides above – in the heavens – then the places on Earth closest to the sky have a resonance that inspires awe. Sacred mountains are revered in many cultures.

The Incas made sacrifices, of both animals and humans, on mountain-tops, and the Mesoamericans built many of their temples on high land. In ancient Iranian mythology, the sacred Mount Alburz was home to the sun god Mithra and the sun and moon revolved around it – it was said to have been the first mountain made when evil irrupted into the cosmos.

The Himalayan peak Mount Kailash, which lies in western Tibet, is sacred in the traditions of Hindus, followers of the indigenous Tibetan Bon religion,

and to Buddhists both Tibetan and non-Tibetan. They identify it with the mythological Mount Meru or Sumeru.

It is on the slopes of Kailash, some Hindus say, that the god Shiva sits cross-legged as a *yogi* on a tigerskin and supports the entire universe by the burning power of his meditation. Buddhists claim that the Buddha himself made the peak holy by descending there with a retinue of 500 followers; its snows are said to have healing properties.

In Chinese myth the sacred peak of Mount Kunlun rose in

the far west, giving issue to the wind and the life-giving waters and linking Earth and sky like Mount Meru; associated with the actual Kunlun range, the mountain was home to the deities Xi Wang Mu (Queen Mother of the West), the Lord of the Rain and the Lord of the Sky.

Mount Kailash in western Tibet, the eastern sacred place of purity, power and transcendence. People of several religions pay their respects to the mountain by circuiting it as part of their acts of personal renewal.

23

In China the creator Pan Gu, who used his energy to burst the cosmic egg (see page 12), struggled for 18,000 years to separate Heaven and Earth and then died, his body becoming China's five sacred mountains, his body hair the vegetation and his breath the winds.

In India, myths of Purusha – the cosmic man with 1,000 heads whose body became the universe – emphasized that he was sacrificed in a sacred ritual like that performed for untold generations by *brahmin* priests. The priests of the Vedic era explained that the act of creation was itself a sacrifice and that in their rituals they not only commemorated this sacred beginning of all things but also maintained the universe as the creator had intended. In the myth the sacred *vedas* (scriptures) were a byproduct of this act of immolation.

In Kiribati, Micronesia, a divine spider with dual form – Old Nareau and Young Nareau – was responsible for creation: Old Nareau fashioned the gods and Young Nareau killed the oldest of them, Na Atibu, and made the universe from the deity's vast body.

In Norse myth Odin and his brothers made the Earth from the giant Ymir, whose body had been formed from the meltwater of the primordial ice. According to the Mesopotamian *Enuma Elish*, Marduk killed his relative Tiamat, the female half of the great creator who had made the gods, and from the two halves of her snake-like body he made the sky and the Earth.

Extant but Shapeless

In ancient Persian tradition, the Earth existed from all time, absolutely flat and formless beneath a stationary sky and surrounded by a calm sea, until evil irrupted into the cosmos, its impact creating the mountains and valleys. At the place where it first struck the Earth towers the sacred Mount

Alburz (see page 23). The event brought movement to the planets and created water in the atmosphere, which in turn formed the cosmic ocean of Vourukasha and fed life on Earth.

This understanding that the Earth always existed but took its present form and was filled with life in the wake of a cataclysmic event informs the Dreamtime creation mythology of Australia's Aborigines. In the Dreamtime, ancestral spirits in the form of great serpents, kangaroos, crocodiles and other creatures gave shape to a formless Earth; for the Aborigines, the Dreamtime moment of creation was an enduring state that could be accessed through ritual.

The most universal of these Aboriginal ancestral spirits was the Rainbow Snake (see page 26), associated with waterholes and winding rivers. In many African traditions, too, creation was linked to a vast serpent identified with the rainbow and life-giving waters. Snakes are found near

waters and so linked to them, while their phallic associations reinforce their connection to fertility (see pages 74–77). One northern African myth told that in the first days the creator initially made a cosmic snake called Minia, which functioned like the World Tree (see box, pages 20–21), linking the levels of the universe, with its tail in the waters beneath the Earth and its head in the sky.

In Africa and elsewhere, creation myths indicate that sky and land were close together in the first days and had to be separated. Just as China's Pan Gu had to prise them asunder, so in Maori mythology Tane, one of the offspring of the sky god Rangi and the earth goddess Papa, had to force his parents apart by inserting himself between them, standing on his head while pushing with his feet against his father; Rangi and Papa have never been reconciled to their separation and their grief is expressed in the tears of rainfall and the mists that rise at daybreak from the earth.

Old Man Coyote and the Ducks

The version of the earthdiver myth told by the Absaroke, a group of Plains Indians widely known as the Crow, featured an intrepid duck as hero.

Before the world, there was water; only the creator, Old Man Coyote, was alive – and he was lonely. So strong was his desire for company that, when he looked on the water, he saw two red-eyed ducks. He spoke to them, suggesting they dive deep to see what they could find.

The first duck dived and for a long time did not return; then, just as Old Man Coyote had given it up for dead, it resurfaced to say it had reached the bottom but brought nothing back. Then it went down again, and when it

returned it had a root in its beak. A third time it swam down, and returned with some mud.

Now Old Man Coyote was mighty pleased with what he saw, and he announced he would use the raw materials to create somewhere to live. He took the earth and blew his quickening breath across it. The lump of mud grew and grew until it formed the great expanse of the North American continent and all the other lands beyond. Then he planted the root, and plants and trees spread across the terrain as

far as Old Man Coyote could see. Pleased with what he had done, he asked the ducks what they thought.

They agreed that the land was fair, but suggested that it needed variety – perhaps mountains and beaches, together with valleys and lakes. With his quick touch Old Man Coyote made the landscape beautiful. Afterwards, he made all the species of animals and the first people, teaching the humans how to hunt, as well as all the other skills necessary for survival.

The First People

A number of cultures imagined the creator as a primeval craftsman who fashioned humankind in the same way a potter might his wares. Other accounts of the appearance of the first humans appear to have been inspired by the wonders of the natural world.

In one Egyptian myth, the god Khnum made the first people from clay on his potter's wheel. One version of the Mesopotamian creation also had the goddess Nammu, helped by the goddess Ninmah, making the earliest humans from clay. In Africa the Shilluk of Sudan accounted for race by suggesting that the creator used various muds – black, brown and white – to make distinct peoples. The Incas said that the creator Ticci Viracocha made the peoples of the Andes from clay and then painted on their clothes in diverse colours, which explains why there are striking differences in the traditional dress of neighbouring areas.

In China Pan Gu was sometimes said to have made the first people from mud, as was the goddess Nu Wa. In other versions, when Pan Gu's body became the world, the fleas that leaped upon it transformed into the first people. One Greek myth had the first people made from clay, in the image of the Olympian gods, by the Titan Prometheus. Similar images reappear in the creation myths of farflung peoples including the Maori, where people are made from sand.

The Aboriginal Arrente of central Australia held that the first people were freed by sky gods from the earth, where they existed in a form not fully realized. The gods, named the Numbakulla Brothers, saw the half-formed people in the mud and came down from the sky with stone knives to cut them free and give them the familiar form of two-legged, ten-fingered humans.

Of Eggs and Water

A number of stories about the first people reflected the earlier Earth-creation stories. Eggs played a prominent role in those tales, so it is not surprising to find a number of myths describing people also emerging from eggs. In the Admiralty Islands of Melanesia, humanity was born from a turtle's eggs laid on the surf-battered beach. One Tibetan myth reported that the first man emerged from the cosmic egg itself, while in the same country's celebrated Epic of Gesar it was claimed that the six clans of ancient Tibet came from birds' eggs that were broken open by divine blacksmiths sent by the gods. In the Greek myth of the goddess who emerged from chaos (see pages 11–12), humanity as well as other life came from the cosmic egg.

Other peoples told emergence myths centred on water. The Chibcha of the Colombian Andes said that the first woman emerged from a mountain lake, having already given birth to the first boy – they became incestuous lovers and spawned the human race. One tradition of the Incas held that the first people came from Lake Titicaca, just as in Africa the Yao of the Lake Malawi region spoke of the first people coming from freshwater lakes.

An Earth Emergence

The idea that the first people emerged from the fertile earth itself was common, particularly among Native American groups. The Hopi, Navajo and other groups from the American southwest told how primeval men came up from a shadowy underworld – like the crops they nursed out of the arid soil (see story box, page 29).

A depiction of a Rainbow Snake, for most Aborigines the primordial deity from whom everything stems. Many stories tell how the snake swallowed the first people, then regurgitated them later in order to populate the landscape – possibly a metaphor for the transition of life from one existence to another.

In western Africa the Ashanti similarly claimed that their ancestors climbed onto the surface of the Earth from an underworld realm. Amazonian Indians including the Caraja and the Guayaki told much the same tale.

In all these emergence myths the Earth is celebrated for its fertility and its likeness to the childbearing mother. For peoples who practised burial rather than cremation or exposure of the dead, the Earth was also the place where their ancestors went – in many cultures the location for the underworld of the dead. As seeds are broken and give issue to shoots, so new life came from the underground realm of the dead. Pueblo peoples of the American southwest built underground ceremonial chambers, where they would perform rituals and recount their creation-emergence narratives before climbing out into the upper sunlight.

Belief in a cave origin was common to many American peoples. Here seven tribes of Aztec ancestors are shown emerging from the womb of Mount Chicomoztoc ("Seven Caves"). The priest striking his staff outside is enacting a symbolic act of creation to bring forth the people.

The World Around

African tradition was rich in tales of the first people emerging from plants. For the southern African Zulu and Tsonga peoples, the earliest ancestors came from a reedbed. The Herero of Namibia said that their ancestors climbed down from a tree, with the first cattle as companions. The pygmy hunters of Central Africa's forests recounted that the first man and woman emerged from a tree trunk after being freed by a chameleon. The Keraki of New Guinea, meanwhile, said the primordial being Gainji discovered the first people chattering high in a palm tree and set them down on the ground.

In ancient Persian tradition, the primeval man Gayormartan was slain by demons, and on his death his semen passed into the earth where it grew into a rhubarb tree. From the tree climbed down the first man and woman, Mashya and Mashyanag, and they gave issue to the generations of men and women that followed.

In the northern Andes, some groups said that the first people and animals grew from seeds made by the god Sibu, but a few myths suggested that the creator had sexual intercourse of some sort and that the fruit was the human race. Sangpo Bumtri, the procreative god of Tibet's Bon religion, had intercourse with a fair consort of turquoise named Chulcam Gyalmo. Their offspring were first the animals and birds, and then the Nine Males and Nine Females of the world – who in turn gave rise to the generations of gods and humans.

Less commonly, particular races were said to be descended from animals. In Tibet, one myth maintained that people were descended from a monkey that coupled with a rock ogress from the Himalayas on the instructions of the bodhisattva Avalokitesvara. The Mongols believed that their ancestors were the children of the blue-grey forest wolf and a doe that ranged the steppes.

The Gifts of Spider Woman

The Hopi claim their ancestors were led from an underworld realm to their home in the American southwest by their creator, Spider Woman, who then taught them all they would need to prosper.

In the beginning, before this world existed, two deities lived together in the underworld: Tawa, the sun god, and Spider Woman, the earth goddess.

Both wished for company and from Tawa emerged Muiyinwuh, the god who controlled the life force, while from Spider Woman came the goddess Huzruiwuhti, keeper of the forms of life. She and Tawa made love, and from their union came great things, including the quarters of the world and the expanses of Above and Below.

Tawa and Spider Woman then shared a sacred thought – to make the Earth and creatures for it. By the power of their thinking and the magic of their singing, they created. Tawa expressed the thought of fishes and running animals; Spider Woman said the thought should have life and made the creatures from clay, placing them beneath a sacred blanket. Then she sang a song to give them life.

The first man and the first woman followed – but when the gods tried to bring them to life with the blanket the sacred rite did not have the desired effect. So Spider Woman rocked them in her arms while Tawa bathed them with his light until breath entered their lungs.

In the world above the first land had not yet appeared from the waters that stretched in all directions. Tawa climbed into the sky, and his magnificent light brought land into being.

The first Indians had become many and in her underworld realm Spider Woman gave them their place and tribal names. Then she took them through the four caverns of her world to a hole that led into the new land above. Following Spider Woman, the first generation of people climbed through and emerged alongside the Colorado River. On her instructions, each clan followed an animal to its appointed territory. Then, before leaving, Spider Woman taught the Hopi their way of life.

How Things Came to Be

Mythologies worldwide are rich in stories of how everyday things came to be the way they are. From myths accounting for the position and movement of the planets and stars in the sky to simple tales explaining why animals look as they do or behave in certain ways, the narratives are marked by great wit and imagination.

In Africa the San of the Kalahari Desert said that Sun lived on Earth among men until a gang of children caught him sleeping and threw him into the sky. Many Native Americans told similar tales tracing the origins of the bright celestial bodies in a familiar life among Earth's mortals.

The Navajo believed that their own ancestors had voyaged upwards through four dark underworlds before they reached the "fifth world" where they lived now; Sun-man and Moon-man came with them and the Navajo threw these fellow travellers up into the sky. In South America the Toba said that the sun was once a woman, who had to flee the unwelcome attentions of a suitor and still runs from him, always heading west; by night she returns to the east through an underground passage. The Iroquois told how the stars of the Pleiades were a group of seven dancing children who floated up into the night sky after their parents refused to feed them in a vain attempt to stop their activities.

An Australian Aboriginal tale claimed that the four pointers of the Southern Cross constellation were the daughters of a great chief, Mululu; they climbed to Heaven to join him after his death.

According to Chinese mythology, the Milky Way was once an earthly river that separated the realms of gods and men, but after a divine weaver fell in love with a cowherd, Xi Wang Mu, Queen Mother of the West, lifted it into the heavens.

The marks people thought they could discern on the face of the moon gave rise to a large body of myth (see box opposite). In Europe, the "Man in the Moon" was sometimes identified as the Biblical Judas, banished for his betrayal of Christ. Elsewhere, explanations were equally fascinating: in a number of tales from the Americas the "Man in the Moon" was sent there for committing incest with his sister; in Inuit myth the male Moon tried to commit incest with his sister Sun but she marked him as punishment – hence the pattern on his face. In New Guinea, the marks were said to be the fingerprints of mischief-loving boys who removed the moon from a container in which it was kept by an old woman, and were then unable to stop it floating away into the heavens.

The Staple Foods

Most peoples related tales of how their staple food originally came to them. Some believed it to have been the work of a culture hero (see page 32), a wondrous figure from long ago who had first instructed their ancestors in particular, precious skills. For the Chinese, it was Shen Nong, divine ancestor and Lord of the Earth, who introduced them to the Five Grains – barley, hemp, two types

Best known in Native American mythology as a great Earth-creator figure, the turtle was said by the Iroquois to have also brought the sun and moon into the world. Afterwards the turtle got the burrowing animals to make holes in the sky to allow the heavenly bodies to disappear, thus providing day and night. Turtle motif on a Native American shield, 19th century.

of millet and vegetables such as beans. Among the Native American Apache the legendary being known as Turkey was revered for having brought forth seeds, fruits and vegetables from his body.

Crops growing from a buried body was also a common motif. The Malagasy of Madagascar told that a mother mourning her dead daughter was instructed by the High God to bury the child in marshland – and from the corpse grew their staple, rice. Such myths celebrated the Earth both as a source of life and home to the dead. In Melanesian myth Sido gave humankind fish, and in one version when he buried his wife the food plants grew from the parts of her body.

Other tales suggested that the first crops emerged thanks to ancestral influence or some other friendly force in the underworld realm. According to the Dayak of Borneo, the souls of the ancestors were transformed into sweetly falling dew that gave life to the ears of rice. The South American Jivaro people told that once there lived a boy who could create their staple, manioc, merely by calling its name, but that his mother allowed him out of her care and he was killed. She was banished to the underworld but there she dances, pushing up the manioc through the soil.

A variant told by the Mikasuki of Florida reported that an old woman rubbed corn from the side of her body to feed her grandsons; when they discovered and were horrified, she told them she would leave, but from her grave underground would continue to push up the corn. Whenever people gathered to eat, they would remember her.

The Gift of Animals

Game and pasture animals were equally vital to people's livelihoods. The Masai of East Africa said that the first cattle had been sent by the sky god down a strip of hide hanging from the heavens. Elsewhere in Africa the Fulani, the Shilluk and the Nandi all maintained that the first cattle came from the waters of a river or lake.

By Arctic tradition, seals, whales and walruses sprang from the severed fingers of the Sea Mother

Rabbit in the Moon

Countless stories were told around the world to account for the vague markings on the face of the moon. In Europe a "Man in the Moon" was the most common explanation, but in places as far apart as China and Mesoamerica a rabbit or hare was seen.

According to Mesoamerican mythology, the moon once shone as brightly as the sun, until a rabbit was sent to dim its luminance and provide a gentle light for the hours of rest.

The ancient Chinese saw the moon's markings as a white hare that prepared the potion of immortality in a vat. A later myth told how when the divine archer Yi was deprived of his immortality by Di Jun, he flew to the palace of Xi Wang Mu, the Queen Mother of the West, and was granted his request for a tablet to make him immortal once more; however, his wife Heng E ate the tablet and, becoming a goddess, rose to the moon, where she took up residence alongside the white hare.

Many images of the rabbit in the moon survive in Aztec and Maya manuscripts, as well as in pottery from the southwestern United States. Artwork based on a detail from the Aztec *Florentine Codex*, 16th century.

– an orphan girl, called variously Sedna, Nuliajuk or Takanakapsaluk, who was mistreated by children or, in another version, killed by her father angry that she had rejected his preferred suitor. According to North America's Chiricahua Apache, animals were created when culture hero Child of the Water took pieces of a slain antelope and blew on them, naming the species as he did so.

A myriad of other creatures, besides those upon which humans depended, featured in another genre of myth: imaginative tales told the world over as to how animals gained distinctive features or behavioural traits. These might take the form of narratives about animal tricksters (see page 66) or culture heroes: for example, widespread myths in the Arctic and Subarctic celebrated how Beaver-man made the wilderness safe by killing a race of giant beasts that lived there and then assigning to their offspring their future size and characteristics. But most such tales, like the African ones of how the leopard got its spots or how dogs became domesticated (see story box opposite), were light-hearted accounts intended to entertain an audience.

The origin of fire was not uncommonly attributed to animals, often as the result of a theft (a scenario familiar to Western readers through the actions of Prometheus – see page 52). In one Arctic myth, the bear was keeper of the world's only flint until the mouse burrowed into the great beast's fur, found the flint and flung it to his partner in crime, the cunning fox, who escaped with it, broke it up and shared the pieces among all creatures. In North America the Cherokee maintained that a water spider brought a live coal back from the first fire, which the gods had jealously hidden in a

sycamore tree. In Africa the Ila people of Zambia recounted that an insect named the mason wasp flew to Heaven and brought fire back to the grateful inhabitants of Earth.

Ancient and Accidental Heroes

As each generation of humans learned the skills necessary for civilized life and for survival in their environment, they were told myths of individual benefactors from long ago, sometimes said to be ancient rulers, or even gods or demi-gods (see pages 80–83). What these so-called "culture heroes" deliberately taught was vital for the maintenance of life.

Instruction in the art of hunting or farming were popular gifts of culture heroes. The Mongo-Nkundo of the Congo basin celebrated Lonkundo, who instructed them in tracking and hunting skills. Half a world away, Patagonian Indians revered El-lal, who taught them to hunt and to use fire, as well as making the land safe by killing a man-eating giant named Goshy-e.

Throughout the Arctic and North America, animal figures such as Hare, Raven, Coyote, Crow and of course Beaver-man, acted as culture heroes

A Yupik dancing mask in the form of a walrus, from the Arctic region. One version of the Sedna story related that, after the girl's hands were hacked off as she clung desperately to the boat she had been thrown from, seals grew from her fingertips, walruses from the rest of her fingers and whales from her hands and wrists. Her corpse sank to the seabed to become Sedna.

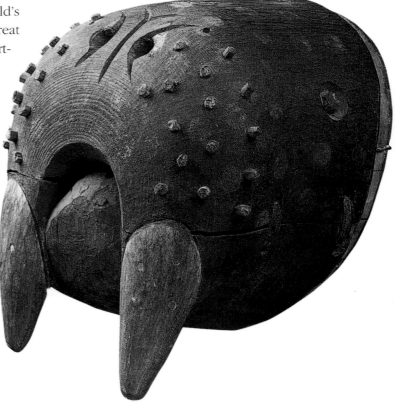

32

A Dog's Life of Ease

Once Jackal and Dog lived as kinsmen deep in the bush. When they passed by the villages of the Mbundu people, they smelled the rich odours of meat cooking and saw men and women squatting around blazing fires.

Jackal wanted fire for himself, so that he and Dog could also cook their meat. He therefore sent Dog into the village to fetch it.

When Dog arrived he ran up to a hut where a woman had finished feeding her child and was scraping the cooking pot. She had leftovers to spare and she fed them to Dog. He ate and found they tasted good – and he understood that life in the village with food aplenty would be better than roaming the bush with Jackal, where most days hunger ruled. So Dog stayed put.

In the bush Jackal howled, as he does to this day, lamenting the fact that Dog had abandoned him and settled down with the villagers. Jackal never got fire, and now is frightened by it. He roams, hunting and scavenging, and has to eat his meat raw.

by transforming elements of the original creation, bringing valuable gifts to their people and making the land safe by outwitting evil monsters. These animals were more commonly encountered in their trickster guise as breakers of rules and disturbers of the status quo (see pages 66–69). When they acted as culture heroes, it was typically their crafty or mischievous actions which unintentionally helped humankind.

In one version of Beaver-man's giant-killing feat in Alaska, for example, his defeated victim rose into the heavens as the sun. The Caddo reported that Coyote slowed the sun down because it was moving too fast across the sky and the days were over too quickly. Travelling with the fiery ball, he asked it to wait while he relieved himself in some bushes – and then never returned, so delaying the sun and prolonging the day.

Culture heroes were sometimes also creators. Among the Chukchi of Siberia, Big Raven made the land, sea and all creatures, and later taught the first people how to propagate by means of sex.

The sun god Bochica appeared from the east among the Chibcha of what is now Colombia and taught the Indians how to make clothes, to cultivate the land and to organize society. He was accompanied by his wife, Chia, who tried to undermine his work, teaching the people only to dance, be merry and have sex; she became their goddess of drunkenness and licence.

Essentials of life, such as fire and light, were gifts commonly bestowed by culture heroes. For South America's Makiritare people, Iureke and Shikiemona killed the toad Kawao, mistress of fire, in order to free the flame that she kept within her body. To escape the wrath of her husband, the jaguar, they hid the fire in the wishu and kumnuatte trees – and even today people rub together sticks from these trees to strike sparks. In a recurrent, well-known Arctic myth – the Tanaina of British Columbia tell it of Hare and the Alaskan Inuit of Raven – the hero freed daylight (or the sun), which had been stolen and hidden away by an unscrupulous chief.

33

The Universal Flood

The tale of a universal flood that sweeps away everyone save a few survivors is probably the world's most widely distributed myth. Rather than originating from a single source, it is more likely that the stories were so common because rising seas, deluges or rivers bursting their banks were frequent occurrences provoking powerful feelings of dread and awe.

In the West, the Biblical tale of Noah is easily the best-known account of a flood that threatened to wipe out the human race. Yet it is far from unique. Many traditions told of a universal flood sent as a result of divine anger. Only in China, where flooding was a commonplace, was the idea that it reflected divine displeasure entirely absent.

In the Mesopotamian myth of Atra-hasis, the god Enlil resolved to destroy humankind because people made too much noise and disturbed him. He sent plagues, drought and finally the deluge. But King Atra-hasis – warned by Enki, the god of wisdom, who was often cast as the protector of humanity – took refuge in a boat with his family and several animals. Atra-hasis survived to honour the gods. In the Assyro-Babylonian version of the myth, the flood survivor was named Ut-napishti, who like Noah was left high and dry on a mountain-top when the waters receded. He was subsequently made immortal for his pains.

In ancient Greek myth, Zeus sent the flood to punish men and women for their wickedness –

A bronze image of mudfish-legged Olukun, the sea god of the Yoruba people, also known as the Lord of the Great Waters. When contesting supremacy with the sky deity Olodumare, Olukun sent a flood to destroy much of the initial creation.

although in some versions it was because he was enraged by Prometheus's insubordination. But Prometheus warned his son and daughter-in-law Deucalion and Pyrrha, who took refuge in a boat, survived the inundation, and were finally deposited atop Mount Parnassus.

A New Creation

The flood myth describes a new beginning, reducing the universe to a state like that of the endless waters of chaos before creation took place (see pages 10–13). In Hindu tradition, the flood was part of the universe's periodic dissolution at the end of each *kalpa* (day) of Brahma (see page 13), ushering in the present age, among others. One version told how when Brahma fell asleep and the scriptures were stolen by a demon, Vishnu came to rescue them. Then Brahma awoke and the age began.

Often the flood begins a second phase of creation, ending a first, flawed universe. The Greenland Inuit told how the flood did away with an earlier world in which people did not die and the Earth became terribly overcrowded; a few survived to inherit the world as people know it now, complete with death. In Maya mythology, the deluge was part of a violent cataclysm that swept away an initial creation in which people were made from wood. The Incas reported that the creator, Viracocha, first made a race of giants to inhabit the Earth, but he grew angry with them; he turned some to stone – and they survived in the form of the vast statues found at Tiahuanaco, Peru – but the rest he swept away by flood. In an Aboriginal myth told by the Worora of Kimberley, ancestral spirits named the Wandjina (see also page 53) sent a flood in the Dreamtime to make space for the universe that people now inhabit.

Mountain Survivors

A tale that survives in many local variants in the Americas tells how a few people survived not in an ark but by taking refuge on a mountain, which was either so tall that the waters did not reach its summit or else floated magically on the ever-rising flood. The Araucanians of Chile described the flood as a contest between two great snakes, one of which raised the waters while the other lifted the mountain on which the people survived.

In China, where river flooding was a constant threat, there were many legends describing how Yu, Master of Floods, won control of the waters. But there was only one universal-flood myth in which the entire Earth was submerged and the bulk of humanity perished. It featured the mother goddess Nu Wa and her brother-consort Fu Xi in the guise of two peasant children who survived a deluge, sent by the dragon god of thunder, by clambering into a hollowed calabash that floated on the waters. After the flood susbsided, they replanted and repeopled the Earth.

In Indian mythology the previous age was set to end with a destructive deluge, but Lord Vishnu (divinely blue, below) appeared in the form of a fish to Manu, father of humankind, and warned him of the coming flood, telling him to take to a boat with creatures and the seeds of plants. When the waters duly arrived, Vishnu towed the ark to a peak high in the Himalayas. He then rescued the sacred scriptures, killing the demon (bottom, left) who had stolen them from the sleeping Brahma. When Brahma woke, the present age began.

Visions of Renewal

Some cultures envisaged that the world would end in apocalyptic violence, but many more, while accepting the notion of monumental destruction, regarded life as an intricate cycle in which the end of one age marked the birth of another, often better, epoch.

Mongolian mythology predicted that the martial god Erlik Khan would burst with nine mounted iron warriors from his underworld realm and destroy all in his path. Erlik, originally the morning star Venus, had been ousted from the heavens at the beginning of time and become King of the Underworld. For the Mongols, as for the Aztecs of Mesoamerica, when the existing universe was brought to an end it would cease to exist forever. There would be no new beginning, no age of peace or glory after the apocalypse.

The Aztecs believed that humankind lived in the last of five ages. They were called "suns" because each was governed by a deity who became the sun of that epoch and who brought

the universe to destruction as the age ended; the fifth sun, in which they lived, was under the rule of Tonatiuh. As in many mythologies, they thought their own age was particularly marked by violence and bloodshed; it would end in an earthquake that would bring time to a shuddering halt.

According to the Aztecs, years came in what they called "bundles" of fifty-two, and they saw the end of each of these fifty-two-year cycles as the most likely moment for time to stop and the world to end (see page 53). In Zoroastrianism, by contrast, the end of the existing world was a moment to be longed for, because although it would be accompanied by great upheavals it would also result in the material universe being cleansed of

The Fear of Celestial Darkness

The spectacle of a lunar or solar eclipse cast terror into the hearts of early peoples. Most saw in these celestial events an attack by a monster on the deity of the sun or moon.

The Indians knew that this act of the moon passing between Earth and the sun – obscuring the sun – can only occur at a new moon and it was woven into mythology: Soma, god of the sacred soma plant and of the moon, kept sixteen cupfuls of nectar which the gods drank one by one as the moon waned; if, as rarely happened, the sixteenth was taken by the sun god Surya then a solar eclipse followed when the demon Rahu attacked Surya, trying to seize the nectar.

Many Central and South American Indians explained that the moon or sun was attacked by a jaguar. The Tartars, of the Altai mountains in Central Asia, claimed a dark vampire crept from its home on a distant star to attack the celestial body.

Egyptian tradition held that the lunar eclipse – when the Earth comes between sun and moon, casting a shadow that dims the moon's light – was a quarrel between gods. Assuming the form of a black boar, Seth

attacked Horus, the falcon-headed sky god whose right eye was the sun and left the moon, tearing the left eye to pieces.

Another explanation, given in Armenia, was that two dark celestial beasts – born of a vast primordial ox – periodically lumbered across the sun and moon, causing the darkening.

Arctic and Tahitian traditions, however, declared that these events occurred during the time that Sun and Moon enjoyed sexual intimacy.

evil, ushering in a perfect age in which all things would be filled with the glory of Ahura Mazda. By tradition, a detailed vision of the world's end was granted to Zoroaster himself: it would begin with earthquakes, droughts and eclipses, but then three saviours would be born of virgins and under their successive rule, evil would cede to good. Under the final saviour, Soshyant, there was to be a bodily resurrection of all humanity, followed by a Day of Judgement – those sent to Hell would be purified and brought to wholeness, while the Earth would be healed, its evil contamination driven out. The apocalypse at the end of time was the fulfilment of the Wise Lord's original plans for his creation, for the universe would then at last find the form he had intended for it, the one it would have taken long ago had not evil rushed into it. Material and spiritual worlds would be perfectly united.

Ash-laden clouds, glowing red, billow apocalyptically from Mount Etna in Sicily during an eruption. However destructive it may seem, both the Earth's existing land areas and its new ones owe their existence to volcanic action.

Tibetan Buddhist tradition similarly envisions a violent cataclysm at the end of the current age that will be followed by a golden age: a 1,000-year era of world peace and enlightenment when the ways of Buddhism will find favour in all countries. According to the Tibetan Buddhist apocalypse vision, an evil ruler will conquer the entire world in the last days, then seek out and besiege the spirit kingdom of Shambhala – which is traditionally believed to exist both in the real world, somewhere in the wastes of the frozen north, and in a parallel spiritual dimension. Then the last king of Shambhala, Rudrachakrin, will ride forth and use

37

his awesome spiritual force to defeat evil. Peace will follow. (In a parallel Tibetan-Mongolian tradition, the hero Gesar of Ling will arise, bringing peace, when evil threatens the end of Buddhism.)

For the ancient Egyptians the end of the universe was not some distant event but a constant possibility that was averted on a daily basis. Each night the sun god Re, or Amun-Re, had to defeat Apophis, the serpent god associated with darkness, evil and trickery. The universe depended on cosmic order – the right balance of good and evil. Ever since humanity had first walked the banks of the River Nile, Re had won the necessary victory, but if one day he were to lose, or even if Apophis were to be killed, thus destroying the balance between good and evil, the universe would come to an end. Then all would be returned to primeval chaos, to the waters of Nun. The gods themselves would be no more, save the One – called Atum in Heliopolis – who was existent before all things. Creation would have come full circle.

Norse mythology's celebrated and detailed vision of the end of the universe described the final hours of both gods and men: its name, Ragnarok, meant "destiny (or doom) of the gods". As in the Aztec vision, the Norse apocalypse was an inevitability from which there was no final escape, but the dread hour could be kept at bay. For example, part of the final onslaught would be the sailing of Naglfar, a ship made from dead men's finger and toenails, and ensuring that people did not die with long nails was considered a vital contribution to postponing this eventuality.

But in contrast to the Aztec vision, the Norse Ragnarok was not an absolute end, for the destruction contained within it the seeds of a new beginning. The great World Tree Yggdrasill (see page 20) would survive the destruction, as would some of the gods, including Odin's sons Vidar and Vali. A new sun, the daughter of the sun of this world, would arise to illumine the skies, and two humans, Lif and Lifthrasir, would emerge from Yggdrasill and people the Earth once more.

In Hindu tradition the coming dissolution of the universe is part of a vast, unending cycle of creation and destruction: time, it is believed, runs forever like a wheel centred on and moved by the divine consciousness or *brahman* that lies beneath and in all things. In the Hindu conception, nothing can be beyond or come after *brahman*, which existed before and after all things – there can be no divine end of the sort envisaged in Norse mythology. As Krishna, embodying *brahman*, says in the *Bhagavad Gita* ("Song of the Lord"), "I am the beginning, the staying and the end of creation".

Hindus nevertheless have their own detailed vision of the world's end. As in many cultures, the current age – called by Hindus the Kaliyuga, or Age of Kali – is traditionally said to be one of wickedness. As the end approaches, oppression will weigh heavily on the people, and the Earth will suffer great degradation. The Kaliyuga will end, it is said, in a 100-year drought as Lord Vishnu, working through the thirsty sun, deprives the Earth of waters. In some accounts, Vishnu will appear astride a white horse and carrying a flaming sword. A vast conflagration throughout the three worlds of Hindu cosmology (see page 18) will be followed by an almighty flood that will return the universe to its primeval, watery state. Then the divine consciousness – cast by different sects in the form of Brahma, the creator, or Vishnu, the preserver – will sleep, resting on the great serpent of eternity, Ananta-Shesha. When the creator awakes, a new creation will begin.

The cycle that will have temporarily come to an end is set within other, immeasurably larger cycles of time as it is experienced by Brahma. By tradition the Age of Kali is the last of four ages, together making up one *mahayuga* ("great age"). A full 1,000 *mahayugas* make up one day for

Brahma, and Brahma is said to live for 100 years. At the end of 100 Brahma years – 155,520 billion Earth years – Brahma will himself die, but after a similar period of chaos a new Brahma will emerge to begin a new cycle.

The Earth Laid Waste

A constant theme in visions of the world's end is that the final days will be preceded not only by moral decline and war but also by a time of dreadful environmental degradation. The Norse Ragnarok was to be ushered in by a winter in which both sun and moon would be swallowed by wolves, and then by an earthquake that would send the trees tumbling. Droughts, crop failures and celestial disturbances attend the end of the current age in both the Hindu and Zoroastrian visions.

The Hittites, creators of a great empire in Anatolia in the second millennium BC, were profoundly moved by the dreadful idea of the Earth abandoned by its native deities and left infertile. In a major myth, the god of agriculture, Telipinu, took offence when his worship was neglected and went into hiding, bringing chaos to Earth and Heaven. However, Hannahanna, the Mother Goddess, managed to mollify his anger, and he returned in peace to rule his domain of the fields. As in the Zoroastrian vision, the Earth was cleansed and healed and so made ready for a new beginning.

An 11th-century statuette of Shiva dancing the Tandava as he destroys the world at the end of an age. In one hand he holds the flame of destruction, in another the *damaru* or drum with which he summons up a new creation. The dance is a symbol both of Shiva's glory and the eternal movement of the universe.

39

WORSHIPPING THE HEAVENS

The earliest humans were animistic; they regarded the phenomena of the natural world with divine awe, making celestial veneration, of sun, moon, planets or stars, one of the oldest forms of religion. The sun in particular was central to the construction of many prehistoric monuments and played an important role in a number of ancient, state-promoted cults. Common to many cultures and faiths was the identification of earthly rulers with solar deities, who were usually male and often related or married to female, lunar ones. So the Egyptian sun god, known by different names in the nation's various centres of power, was believed to rule over the heavenly kingdom; this orderly state of affairs was replicated on Earth in the person and reign of the pharaoh. The myths explained how this situation arose and why it had to be maintained. Similar beliefs were found elsewhere around the world. In Peru the ruling Inca was believed to be the sun incarnate (Inti, son of the creator god) and his wife the moon; in Japan genders were reversed, and the ancestor of the first human emperor was the sun goddess Amaterasu, married to her brother, the moon god Tsukiyomi; in Indonesia the royal princes were descended from the sun; and in Persia the religion of Mithraism, transported by Roman legionaries to Europe, celebrated the Unconquerable Sun of the military emperors.

Above right: In ancient India the Vedic sun god, Surya, was a powerful symbol of universal energy as well as the source of light and warmth. In the miniature painting, *Heart of Surya*, 1725, Vishnu and his consort Lakshmi bask in his comforting glow.

Right: The standing stones of England's Stonehenge at twilight. The site evolved from a Neolithic sepulchre, *c.*3000BC, oriented to the midwinter full moonrise, to become a Bronze Age temple aligned to the midsummer sunrise, *c.*2000BC.

In early times the existence of the two great heavenly bodies, one visible by day, the other by night, led people to speculate that the universe was ordered by contrasting principles, with pairs of opposites regulating life's flow. The powerful and fiery sun was usually seen as male, the beauty of the moon as female; the two were frequently regarded as husband and wife or even brother and sister. The nurturing, life-giving qualities of sunlight were fundamental to agriculture, while the lunar cycle emphasized the predictable, recurring rhythms of life, death and rebirth. Myths gave the moon the power to govern all essential change; it thus not only became associated with human fate and behaviour, but its periodic disappearance led to taboos against undertaking any creative actions on Earth during that period. Geography was a factor too: Earth's axial tilt is such that the sun is absent for much of the year in the far north, so in Arctic cultures the moon, unusually, came to assume an importance rivalling that of its fiery daytime counterpart.

Above: Japan's sun goddess Amaterasu married her brother Tsukiyomi, god of the moon. But she fell out with him and the pair were seldom seen together. Yoshitoshi's 19th-century print, from the series "One Hundred Aspects of the Moon", shows the warrior-monk Benkei under Tsukiyomi's gaze and at the mercy of the third sibling deity, the storm god Susano.

Left: Gold was prized among West Africa's Akan peoples. Their most revered artifact was the Golden Stool, said to have been conjured from the sky by priests as proof of celestial power and blessing. Stylized gold head of a female, 19th century.

Below: Diana, Roman goddess of the hunt, depicted with her followers, the "lunatics" or moon-worshippers. Diana was associated with the goddess Luna (Greek Selene or "moon", sister of the sun god Helios), to whom people offered prayers at new and full moons. Illustration from a Parisian edition of a work by Christine de Pisan, *c.*1410.

Left: Hathor, Egyptian goddess of love, beauty and fertility, adorns this mirror's gold-inlaid obsidian handle. Her face and the silver mirror disc both symbolize rebirth, the disc representing the sun, Hathor's father. Tomb of Princess Sat-Hathor-Iunet at Kahun, 12th Dynasty, *c.*1818–1772BC.

Centre: Celestial chariots featured in many mythologies worldwide, including those of Persia, China and India. Here, Arjuna, deity of sunrise and son of the storm god Indra, drives the seven-horsed vehicle of the sun through the sky.

Below: The ornate decor of this Aztec headdress, with its feathers, gold suns, crescents and temple shapes, mark it as a piece of royal or priestly regalia, exuding sacredness and power. The green feathers are male quetzal tail plumes, associated with the life-giving figure of the serpent-bird god Quetzalcoatl. Gold metalwork links it to the solar deities, particularly the god of war and the sun Huitzilopochtli, with whom the Aztec leader, Emperor Motecuhzoma, was identified. The Aztecs considered gold to be a product of the sun and silver a gift of the moon.

A WORLD ALIVE WITH GODS AND SPIRITS

The word "animism" was coined by scholars during the nineteenth century to describe a world-view that saw spirits where, by the standards of modern rationalism, they should not be – in objects that by scientific definition are "inanimate". Rivers, mountains, boulders, waterfalls – all for the animist could have souls, and so could storms, rain, the sun, the moon and distant planets. The animists' world was a crowded one, full of invisible but powerful presences that demanded the respectful attention of human beings.

It went without saying that in this world animals had personalities too, and responded to their surroundings much as humans did. Hunting peoples drew from this belief the conclusion that the spirits of their prey needed propitiation. Much like their own human ancestors, the game they killed expected to be treated with respect; if not, the beasts' spirits could cause trouble in the otherworld, a parallel universe of the dead never far from our own.

With the coming of agriculture, human hopes and fears turned on harvesting the crops, and the seasons assumed a central importance both in real life and in the myths that were its reflection. Seminal legends arose around the endless cycle of growth, death and regeneration, seeking to explain why the world comes alive in spring and dies in winter. People saw in that sempiternal pattern divine dramas of murder and abduction, bestowing on the effects of the Earth's axial tilt the full gamut of their own most secret emotions.

Inextricably linked with the notion of restored fertility was the age-old belief in a female principle in nature that expressed itself in the worship of the Great Goddess. Originally the earth itself, she now became personified as its renewer. And while her cult touched some of humankind's deepest roots, a less profound and altogether racier note was struck by tales of tricksters, the jokers in the mythic pack who represented the unchanging realities of human self-seeking and greed.

Finally there were the domestic entities who stood guard over hearth and home. For even in people's most private sanctuaries, the unseen spirit world called for consideration. This realm was always a challenging place, full of traps for the unwary. Only by constant alertness could an individual find rest amid its ever-present throng.

Opposite: Hundreds of intricate sculptures adorn the 14th-century marble structures of the Jain Temple of Chaumukha at Ranakpur, India.

Below: A stylized eagle from an Anglo-Saxon shield, *c.*AD665. The bird was a symbol of the pagan god Woden or Odin, chief deity of the Germanic pantheon. Woden was linked to the heavens and, in snake form, to the underworld; he was also associated with magic and warfare.

Powerful Spirits of Place

For many early peoples, supernatural forces were everywhere – in mountains, rivers, lakes, forests, even unusually shaped boulders or trees. Such spirits had significant power, and the wise took care not to ignore or offend them.

The Romans called them *genii loci*, spirits of place, but they were already old by the time that Rome was founded. It may even be that these localized divinities were the world's first gods. Certainly the belief in a universe full of hidden power lies at the roots of many of the world's great religions.

But the awe that early humans felt in face of the outside world was very different from modern, romantic notions of Mother Nature. The original instinct was less one of serene contemplation than of terror. In undeveloped societies, the physical environment was at best a fickle friend, at worst a place of mortal danger where disaster in the form of famine, flood or attack by wild animals was never very far away. In such circumstances, nature worship was more a constant struggle to appease fierce gods than a quest for spiritual tranquillity. For Polynesian islanders, for example, the world about them was alive with menacing spirits. The Maori called them *tipua*, and even mentioning their name could be dangerous. Travellers passing a spot where one lived would seek to placate it by making an offering of a twig or reciting a chant.

At the other end of the globe, the Arctic's icy wastes were equally threatening, and there too people travelled cautiously in a world of baleful presences. Some areas were considered perpetually unlucky, and hunters would make substantial detours to avoid places where accidents had happened, fearing that they were the haunts of evil spirits. And in Europe, the Slav world also was full of malign entities that could be lethal if they were not properly propitiated. Farmers in some parts kept a one-hour curfew at noon to avoid alienating the white-cloaked *poludnitsa*, a much-feared female spirit who thought no more of lopping off a farmer's head than of cutting ears of corn.

Yet the spirits that animated the landscape could also be sources of strength. Australian Aborigines used the concept of *djang* to express the power that was latent all around them, but especially so in certain sacred spots. In Aboriginal mythology, this was the creative energy that shaped the earth in the legendary first era known as the Dreamtime. Stories passed down the generations spoke of the adventures of primeval culture heroes – the Rainbow Snake, the Wawilak Sisters, Opossum Woman – in shaping the environment. These great creators left some of their own power in the marks they left behind them. Even now people seek to reconnect with it through rituals and dances, or perhaps just by touching a stone at a spot where the heroes once toiled or rested.

Guardians of the Waters

Other cultures had tales of the occasional generosity of individual spirits. There were several African legends of girls thrown supposedly to their death in rivers, who in fact were rescued through the intervention of the supernatural guardians of the stream (see box, pages 48–49). Similar stories in China told of the blessings bestowed on certain lucky individuals who happened to win the favour of the dragon kings thought to live in underwater palaces on the beds of lakes and rivers.

Water spirits were actually an unusually volatile group, perhaps reflecting the changeable aspect of the element in which they lived. There

An important part of Celtic religions was an association between water and spiritual power, reflected in the veneration of certain springs, lakes and rivers. Wooded sites, similar to this one on the River Doe at Ingleton in Yorkshire, were particularly potent.

were fearsome creatures like the *klu* that inhabited Tibetan lakes and streams, or the deadly *rusalka*, mermaid-like sirens who lingered in pools in the Slavic lands to lure unwary travellers to a watery grave. But there were also friendly nymphs, including the beautiful Naiads of classical myth or the spiritually powerful *kami* who occupied Japanese rivers; it was common there for mystically inclined ascetics intent on acquiring the

powers of a shaman to spend hours meditating in mountain streams or under waterfalls, even in the freezing depths of winter.

One sub-group of particularly benevolent spirits were the healing deities who inhabited springs in Celtic lands. Most districts had a source or well where local people would go in search of cures for their ailments. In time some became internationally famous. In France the source of the

The Gift of the River King

A story from Lesotho in southern Africa shows how local spirits could reward good behaviour and punish those who stubbornly refused to comply.

Selekana was a beautiful young woman, and her good looks won her the admiration of all the young men – and the undying hatred of the other village girls. Eventually their envy grew too much to bear, and they decided to get rid of her by throwing her into a neighbouring river.

But Selekana did not drown as they had expected. Instead she was seized by the god of the river, who took the form of a ferocious crocodile. Taking her to his realm on the river-bottom, a magical place where she could live and breathe as easily as in the human world, he set her to work as a servant for his consort, River Woman.

Life was not easy in this underwater domain, for the tasks she had to perform were endless. But she was as patient and industrious as she was pretty, and she did them all without complaining. Her forbearance so impressed River Woman that eventually the spirit decided to let her return to the human world, giving her a gift of precious stones from the riverbed as a leaving present.

Selekana's enemies were startled when she reappeared in the village, and after they had seen the valuable treasures she had brought back with her they were consumed by jealousy too.

Seine – known as the Sequana Spring – was the centre of a temple complex in Roman times, while in Britain people came from all parts to visit the site the Romans called Aquae Sulis, the waters of the god Sulis, which later became the city of Bath.

The magic adhering to water evidently inspired the custom of casting offerings into the depths, known throughout both the Celtic lands and Scandinavia. Archaeological investigations in eastern England in 1982 provided spectacular evidence of the practice at Flag Fen, where more than 300 metal objects, including valuable swords, were found; they had apparently been dropped into the bog from an elaborate artificial island.

Memories of such traditions no doubt lay behind tales of the death of King Arthur, who insisted that his sword Excalibur should be cast into a lake before he could depart in peace. Similarly, the Lady of the Lake who came to carry off his body preserved the memory of the healing water spirits of earlier times. An even hazier memory of the custom of leaving offerings to water spirits still survives in the habit of casting coins into wishing-wells or fountains for good luck.

The Allure of Heights and Hollows

Mountains held quite as much numinous power as water did, and at a time when few people ventured up them it was easy to imagine them as the abode of gods (see box, page 23).

Many cultures had sacred peaks: the ancient Greeks honoured Mount Olympus, the Icelanders Helgafell, the Japanese Fujiyama and the Tibetans Mount Kailash. The Chinese recognized five – one for each of the cardinal directions and the fifth for the centre of the world. In the Americas the Aztecs built several shrines at the top of mountains, the most important of them dedicated to the rain god Tlaloc on the peak that still bears his name. A child was sacrificed there each spring, and the blood used to bathe a statue of the god in the hope of preventing a drought.

Children were also occasionally buried alive in caves, which had a special significance for many Central and South American peoples. The Olmecs, who established the first Mesoamerican culture, carved cave symbols onto their thrones, and for more than 2,000 years thereafter people in the region made pilgrimages to natural shrines in the

Selekana's greatest enemy was the chief's daughter. So covetous was she of her rival's new-found wealth that she promptly resolved to throw herself into the same river in the hope of winning even more beautiful jewels still.

But where Selekana had been patient and forbearing, the newcomer was haughty and uncooperative. When the River King instructed her to serve his wife, she refused point blank. And so the giant crocodile swallowed her up, handing out the summary justice that folktales generally reserved for arrogant, greedy people.

rocks. The largest building constructed in the Americas in early times, the massive Pyramid of the Sun at Teotihuacan in central Mexico, was built over a mound with a cave at its heart. A millennium later, the Aztecs even sometimes cut shrines out of the living rock, apparently in imitation of caverns.

For the Incas of what is now Peru, caves had special significance as openings to the under-world. Their myths told how an earlier human race had disappeared underground; the world was only repeopled when their successors emerged from caverns, which were consequently regarded as places of special spiritual power. They also venerated rocks, for many of the heroes of the re-emergence were said to have been petrified, among them the Inca dynasty's founder, Manco Capac, and his two brothers. Sometimes this odd link between stones and heroes worked the other way: one well-known legend described how the boulders on the hills around their capital, Cuzco, had once come alive to help defeat invaders.

If inanimate rocks could be imbued with spiritual force, so could living trees, which had a special significance among Celtic peoples. Druid priests conducted their ceremonies in groves of trees, and one of their most holy rites involved the cutting of mistletoe from a sacred oak with a golden sickle. According to the Roman historian Tacitus, the Germanic tribes also worshipped in forest glades. In both Germany and Scandinavia, trees were planted outside temples and other important public buildings to serve as guardians and protectors. Something of the magical aura accorded them survived in later stories of magical forests, such as the Broceliande of the Arthurian legends or Shakespeare's Arden. And even today the nation's woodlands have a hallowed place in most German hearts.

In truth, though, there is almost no end to the list of places with spiritual power, for the animistic impulse to find suprahuman forces at work in nature was both archaic and worldwide. So too was the mixture of reverence, awe and terror that its wonders inspired. And, buried deep within that complex web of emotions, lay the source of a multitude of legends and one of the principal roots of myth.

Masters of the Elements

The awe inspired by nature's elemental forces was another wellspring of world mythology. Storms, thunder, rain, fire – all were linked with the gods, and people sought to protect themselves from harm by offering them appropriately respectful worship.

Long before science could predict or explain the workings of the elements, people had to live with their consequences, which could be dire indeed. Storms were terrifying; in their savage violence, cultures all over the world sensed the anger of some superhuman power. Fire was at best a dangerous and unpredictable friend. And rain or the lack of it could mean death and destruction on a massive scale, either in the form of lethal floods or equally devastating droughts.

So the natural impulse was to placate and appease the spirits responsible for these fearsome displays. And as none was more impressive than a raging tempest, it is hardly surprising that in some cultures the storm god took pride of place in the entire celestial hierarchy.

The Fecund Storm Gods

One such was the principal god of the Canaanites, as described in a cache of early tablets found at the ancient site of Ugarit on the Syrian coast. Known simply as Baal or "Lord", like several other deities in the region, he was also referred to in the texts as the Cloud Rider. Myths described him speaking with a voice of thunder and watering the earth through a hole in the floor of his celestial palace – a link that duly led to his worship as a fertility god combatting the Levantine summer drought.

Similar claims were made for Teshub, the great god of the Hittites in the second millennium BC. His link with the fierce storms of the region – around Anatolia, in modern Turkey – led him to be regarded as a war god; but his ferocity had a life-giving goal, for his principal enemies, such as the dragon Illuyankas, represented the sterility of dead land, revivified by Teshub's gift of resuscitating rain.

Teshub had echoes in the Norsemen's Thor, another fighter ready to take on any adversary at a moment's notice. He was god of lightning, wind and rain, and thunder was said to be the rumble of his chariot as it careered across the sky. Although Thor's chosen weapon was the hammer, his Celtic counterpart Taranis (literally "Thunderer") preferred thunderbolts – imaginary divine missiles that were sometimes confused with real-life meteorites. These were also the favoured instruments of Zeus, chief of the Greek pantheon; poets claimed he transported them on Pegasus, the winged horse.

In pagan Russia the thunderbolt-hurler was Perun, the principal deity of the city-state of Kiev. There people identified the bolts with the fossils known as belemnites; noting that these were rarely found immediately after thunderstorms, they explained the delay by claiming that the bolts buried themselves deep in the earth, only re-emerging after the magically significant period of seven years. In later, Christian times, Perun's memory became confused with that of the prophet Elijah (known in Russian as Ilya), who like him was associated with a fiery chariot; until quite recently, peasants hearing thunder would claim that Ilya was chasing demons across Heaven.

In the Americas the best-known storm-creature was the Thunderbird, whose beating pinions created the thunder's rumble and whose eyes flashed forth the lightning. So vast were the birds, the Northwest Coast peoples claimed, that they could carry off whales in their talons. Similar traditions were also known in Asia, where Chinese legends spoke of the Windbird which could raise storms simply by flapping its mighty wings.

The link between storm deities and agricultural fertility, apparent in the myths of Baal and Teshub, was also evident in Indian mythology. This recorded how the god Indra used thunderbolts to slay Vritra, the demon of drought, and so liberated the cloud-cattle which he had corralled in his ninety-nine fortresses. Freed, the beasts stampeded thunderously across the heavens before releasing torrents of life-giving monsoon rain.

Some of the stranger folk-beliefs about rain came from China. It was believed by peasants there that rain was in the gift of the dragon-kings, who could leave their homes in rivers, lakes and seas and mount the clouds to cause downpours. When drought threatened, they would beg them to intervene, taking their images from the temples to show them the parlous state of the crops. In the hierarchical ranking of gods undertaken by Daoist scholars, the dragon-kings' place was taken by a Lord of the Rain whose home was on sacred Mount Kunlun. His colleagues in the heavenly bureaucracy included a Count of the Winds and a Lord of Lightning, while the bird-headed Thunder-god headed a whole ministry of lesser deities charged with the task of punishing crime.

Fire: Friend and Foe

Fire rivalled water in the world's myths, though personifications of the element were comparatively rare. India had a fire-god, Agni, as did the Persians in Atar, who saved the world by driving off the spirit of evil when he attempted to darken the sun. Partly in memory of his action, eternal flames were kept burning in Zoroastrian temples, giving

Black-skinned Krishna, riding on the magical eagle Garuda, confronts Indra in the course of a dispute between the gods, from the epic *Harivamsa, c.*1590. The Vedic god Indra's ascendancy had been secured with the slaying of Vritra, the monster of drought, and his defeat by Krishna, an incarnation of Vishnu, was symbolic of the victory of later gods over the older ones.

rise to the mistaken belief among foreigners that followers of the religion were fire-worshippers, a claim they vehemently denied.

Fire was most often represented in myth as a pre-existing element, often the preserve of the gods, that was brought to Earth by the action of a culture hero (see pages 32–33). For the ancient Greeks the benefactor was Prometheus, who stole fire from the Olympian realm and was horribly punished for his pains; Zeus chained him to a rock in the Caucasus, where an eagle came daily to peck out his liver. Chinese tradition ascribed the introduction of fire to the nation's legendary first

ruler, the Yellow Emperor. For the Maoris, it was stolen by the trickster Maui from the underworld, where the goddess Mahuiike nurtured it in her burning fingernails. American mythology was also rich in fire-stealers, who could often be otherwise humble creatures; for the Opaye of Paraguay, the thief was a guinea-pig that spirited the first flame away from an animal spirit, the jaguar's mother, who was its guardian.

Once on Earth, fire had to be treated with respect. It had special status for the Mongols, whose laws proscribed harsh punishments for all who offended against it, for example by spitting

The Sun's Unwanted Gift

A myth from the Polynesian island of Tonga in the South Pacific warned of the devastating legacy of a union between the sun god and a mortal woman.

Crossing the heavens one day, the sun was attracted by a beautiful, half-naked woman he saw catching fish. He came to her in human form, and nine months later she bore him a son, Sisimatailaa. The boy grew up a handsome youth, and when the time came to marry he had no trouble finding a bride. But he wanted his father's blessing on the union, so at his mother's suggestion he climbed to the top of the island's highest mountain to beg the sun's permission for him to take a wife.

His appeal did not go unanswered. Two bundles dropped down from the sky, and with them came a warning – only one should be opened, while the other must remain untouched. He returned home with the packages, and when he

unwrapped the first he found a treasure of gold and silver inside.

He kept close watch on the other bundle to see the god's instructions were obeyed, and it lay unopened for months. But then one day he and his wife went out together fishing. It was hot, and he dozed; and while he did so, his wife came across the mysterious package. Like her Greek counterpart Pandora, she was consumed by curiosity to know what might be inside, and the consequences of her inquisitiveness were to prove just as dire. For in opening the bundle she released storms and tempests into the world, and she and her husband became their first victims when the savage winds capsized their boat, sending them to a watery grave beneath the waves.

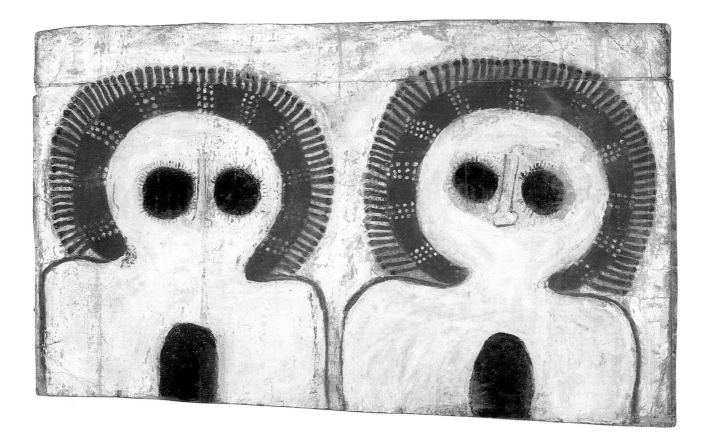

In Australia's Kimberley region, the elements and the natural world's fertility are controlled by ancestral spirit beings known as Wandjina who reside in the sea and sky. Aborigines used fire as a renewal agent to complement the water delivered by the Wandjina, shown here with characteristic cloud halo features.

into a hearth. It was also used by their shamans, both in divination rituals involving the scorching of sheep's shoulder-blades and for purposes of purification; foreigners visiting Mongol dignitaries had to pass between two fires before audiences began.

With similar aims in mind, Slav peasants would drive cattle between fires when an epidemic threatened in the hope of warding off disease. Persian respect for the element extended to the notion of ordeal by fire as a way of determining the truth in disputed legal cases. Survival was taken as divinely bestowed proof of innocence.

Yet maybe the most spectacular celebration of fire in the mythological record came from the Aztecs of Mexico, for whom the element was intimately connected with fears of the end of the world. At the end of each fifty-two-year cycle in their sacred calendar, they conducted a New Fire Ceremony that involved the extinction of all flames in the empire. This was a dangerous time when all life could come to an end, so in the countdown to the fatal hour household goods were smashed and people refrained from food, sex and most usual activities. Normal life came to a standstill.

On the final night, a procession of priests and dignitaries made their way to a mountain-top near the capital of Tenochtitlan, today's Mexico City. There they waited for midnight, while the whole populace below remained frozen in anticipation. The priests' eyes were fixed on the constellation of the Pleiades; if the stars continued to move through the heavens after the crucial hour, it was a sure sign that the world would survive. When the stars duly obliged, an important captive was sacrificed on the peak. Then the priests used a fire-drill to strike a spark, reintroducing fire to a world that had briefly been deprived. A bonfire was lit to spread the good news, and amid general rejoicing the new flame was carried down the mountainside to the city's Great Temple and so to the population at large. Once again the world had survived; and the token of its resilience was the primal flame.

Bonds Between Animals and Humans

In myth there was no clear dividing line between beast and human. Animals interacted, talked and sometimes even mated with people, and those who treated them with due respect were invariably the ones who benefited most from the connection.

Mythology encapsulates ways of thought just as it captures people's deepest ambitions and fears; and there are few areas where these have changed so radically as in regard to the animal world. The modern view of animals as intrinsically distinct from and inferior to humans would have been incomprehensible to early societies, which viewed all life as interlinked. Hunting peoples imitated animals in their rituals to gain something of their special power, and in their myths they drew no clear line between themselves and the other species sharing their lands.

A typical hunting-society rite, in this case from Finland, is described in the nation's epic, the *Kalevala*. It describes the killing of a bear, which was duly butchered and eaten. But the bones were saved and given a solemn burial alongside grave-goods that included skis and a knife. The mourners sang the dead beast's praises, lauding it as a friend and begging it to let its fellow-bears know just how well it had been treated. Then, the assumption went, they too would allow themselves to be hunted in turn, providing a regular

Bulls were among the first animals to be depicted by humans; the many examples found in prehistoric cave art include this one from France. The animals usually symbolized male potency. Zeus took on bovine form to accomplish many acts of seduction, and the Minoans admired the animals' virility, sacrificing bulls in honour of Athene during the annual Panathenaia Festival.

source of provisions for the community. The notion of consent on the part of the victim was a central part of the hunting creed.

Fear played a part in the respect shown to non-human creatures, for in some parts of the world – notably in Siberia and the Americas – prey species fell under the protective embrace of powerful spirits known as Masters of the Animals. These beings were happy for the beasts that came under their care to be killed, but only if the correct procedures and rituals were observed and fitting respect was shown. Woe betide any hunter who killed animals needlessly or who left them to suffer rather than taking them as food. At the very best he could expect the animal's supernatural guardian to withhold game in future, so that he would go home empty-handed; at worst, he could be punished by humiliation or even death.

In Central America, it was commonly believed that the Animal Master lived under a mountain, and that he gathered the creatures of the wild there at nights, just as farmers penned domestic livestock. Legend had it that hunters who merely wounded animals rather than killing them outright could expect to be taken to his hideaway to atone for their misdeeds. There they would be shown all the creatures they had caused to suffer needlessly; and they would not be allowed to quit the place until they had nursed each one back to health.

The Power of Kinship

Beliefs such as these developed out of a profound sense of kinship with the other denizens of the animal kingdom. Early hunters were of course intimately aware of how prey species differed

from the human race: they studied their special strengths and weaknesses, the behaviour patterns that could be exploited to bring them to the kill. But such particularities were ultimately superficial, for underneath they shared the same nature and emotions as those who pursued them, and responded to the same stimuli and the same fears. It went unquestioned too that they had souls, just as people had. So, alive, they could be tempted and cajoled; dead, they needed propitiation, in the

Animal figures adorning this Native American totem pole in Vancouver, British Columbia, served as clan emblems with great ancestral and spiritual significance. The carving acted as a declaration of the links between animal and human, specifically in the genealogy of the individual displaying it. Bears were particularly prized as guardian spirits for their strength and daring; to have one as an ancestral figure was highly sacred.

same way that the spirits of ancestors had to be appeased by the appropriate observances.

A consequence of this sense of consanguinuity was the strange, inter-species fluidity that now seems one of the odder aspects of world myth. In tales from cultures as far apart as North America and Australia, Siberia and the Celtic world, people regularly changed into animals or birds and back. Time and again the species barrier was broken, often without any attempt at logical explanation,

Examples of this trait include the many stories of marriages with animals that take human form. Then there are the animal kinship tales. A typical example comes from the Pawnee people of what is now Nebraska, who recounted how a hunter came across a bear cub one day and spared its life, asking it only that, if he were to have a son, the bears would help him to become wise in their ways. His wife duly became pregnant, and the boy she bore showed an instinctive rapport with bears from an early age.

Then, as a young man, he went out with a war party that was ambushed by rival Lakota warriors; the Pawnee fighters were slaughtered to a man. But bears came upon the corpses and, recognizing the bear-man among the dead, used animal magic to bring him back to life. Then they took him to live with them. He stayed for many years, learning to see life as a bear does. Eventually he went back to his own people and became a great chief, taking care to pass on the bear lore to his descendants and to teach them respect for their animal cousins.

Such stories permeated the world's folklore, evolving in time into the animal-helper theme familiar from fairytales, in which the hero who treats animals he meets kindly is later saved from disaster with their aid. In contrast, characters who treat other species with cruelty or contempt invariably come off badly themselves.

This plotline in fact has great antiquity, as one of the few surviving stories from ancient Egypt shows. It tells how the goddess Isis set out one day protected by an escort of seven scorpions. She stopped for the night at the house of a wealthy woman, but the lady refused to admit her insect companions. Enraged at the insult, the scorpions pooled their venom into a single sting. Its super-lethal owner then found a way into the compound and stung the woman's son. But the story had a happy ending: Isis, a mother herself, could not stand to see the child die and used magical formulas to save his life.

In ancient Egypt cats were ambivalent symbols of both death and fertility; good and bad omens. Such was the strength of the cult of the cat that to kill one was an offence punishable by death. The cat-headed goddess Bastet was personified by a living cat, and upon the animal's death its owner mourned in public, shaved his eyebrows and had the cat mummified. Bronze votive statue, Egypt, c.575BC.

From Divinities to Servants

Ancient Egypt was a centre of animal cults, where certain species seem to have been venerated as tribal divinities in predynastic times. Later, they became identified with specific deities; for example, ibises and baboons were protected by the scribe god Thoth, while the goddess Bastet was the patron of cats. The link with the gods continued after death. Whole mortuaries have been excavated containing the mummified remains of cats, bulls, monkeys, birds, rodents and even insects, each one the representative of a given deity to whom the embalmed body was offered up.

In many other cultures elsewhere, animals were not just respected but were considered sacred. In India, monkeys and cows both benefit still from protected status because of their special standing. The custom's origins are now lost in time, though the *Rig Veda* refers to a mystic relationship between the cow and the earth.

Over time, with the development of agriculture, attitudes towards animals inevitably changed. Although livestock remained essential for their owners' survival, they were under people's control in a way that wild game had never been. Familiarity bred a degree of contempt, and the process of turning living creatures into commodities, brought to fruition by agri-business over the past two centuries, got under way.

Quite simply, animals were disempowered. With their spirit guardians no longer there to protect them, there was no force to preserve them, other than human empathy and charity. Sadly for the world's species, those emotions were to prove very inadequate safeguards.

The Divine Drama of the Seasons

Agricultural societies depend on the regular alteration of rainy and dry spells for their harvests, and so for their survival. So it is comes as no surprise that they dramatized their concerns in tales of warring gods.

Some cultures had relatively uncomplicated myths about the seasons. Certain Inuit peoples, for instance, personified them as two spirits, Nipinouke and Pipounouke, who simply took it in turns to rule the world. Other groups with similar concepts added the notion of conflict. So the Aborigine inhabitants of Groote Eylandt off Australia's northern coast claimed that their rain-god, Bara, was taken captive each April by his enemy Mamariga, the spirit of the hot winds of the dry period. Bara would spend the next seven months each year imprisoned in a hollow tree on a head-land, and during that time all greenery would disappear from an arid world. Then, come November, the people would gather to tempt him out with rites and offerings; and sure enough, the rainclouds would gather soon after and Bara's time of year come round again.

In the Hawaiian islands the equivalents of Mamariga and Bara were Ku and Lono. Myths told how Lono, the venerated god of rain and fertility, distraught with grief at the death of his wife, had long ago left the islands by canoe, but had promised to come back with food. And, sure enough, he did return, every year when the constellation of the Pleiades first became visible in the evening sky. And he brought with him the rains that made the islands fertile.

For four months he was feted by the populace. He was carried in effigy around the islands, always in a clockwise direction, and everywhere he went he was greeted with feasting and celebration. Then, at the end of the growing season, he returned to his home in a temple on the main

A cluster of menacing figures surmount the stone wall at a public temple enclosure site, or *heiau*, near Hanaunau, Hawaii. In local cosmology three prominent gods, Kane, Ku and Lono, formed a trinity and the dry and wet seasons were controlled by the latter two through a process of ritualized warfare. The oversized heads reflect the gods' great *mana* or spirit power.

Relief of a wheatsheaf carved on a lintel, from Eleusis in Greece where a sanctuary or temple to Demeter once existed. Daughter of Rhea, granddaughter of Gaia, sister to Zeus and mother of Persephone, this earth goddesss was associated with a religion based on the mysteries of the cycle of resurrection and rebirth as it was witnessed in agriculture and nature, especially corn.

island. There a ritual was conducted in which he was ceremonially defeated by his enemy Ku, the god of the dry season and of war. Then his image was put away. Lono, it was said, had returned to his distant home in the invisible land of Kahiki.

This myth exploded into history in January 1779 when the English navigator Captain James Cook landed on Hawaii, coincidentally at the time when Lono was expected. He had sailed around the islands to his landfall in the appropriate, clockwise direction, and he brought with him unfamiliar gifts including food. The masts and sails on his vessels even approximated in shape and colour, if not in size, to the ceremonial staffs and banners that usually accompanied the Lono processions. The islanders not unnaturally thought that Lono had sent a living representative that year, or perhaps had even put in a personal appearance.

The mistake was cruelly shown up when, having undergone the annual leave-taking ceremony in the temple, Cook duly left the islands – only to hove back into port shortly after to undertake essential repairs to a damaged ship. For Lono to return in this way so soon after his departure was unheard-of – a disaster that threatened both the seasonal round of growth and harvest and the authority of the island's ruler, who was expected to guarantee the welfare of the community. To his astonishment, Cook found himself greeted with angry recriminations by the very same islanders who had previously feted him; then violence erupted and Cook was stabbed to death.

Tales of Abduction

Other tales of disappearing divinities carried an altogether more complex symbolism. There were, for example, the myths of abducted goddesses whose departure had disastrous effects on the world they left behind. In Norse myth, Idun was the goddess of spring and rejuvenation, guardian of the golden apples of eternal youth. When she and her magical fruit were kidnapped by the giant Thiassi, old age descended on the gods of Asgard and sterility on the earth, only to be lifted when she was rescued by the trickster Loki.

The Greeks told a similar story about Persephone, goddess of spring and the new crop, and her abduction by Hades, god of the underworld. With her disappearance nothing would grow on Earth. Her mother Demeter searched for her frantically, eventually tracing her to the dark realm of the dead. The gods then negotiated her return to the land of the living, only to learn that she had eaten a pomegranate seed in Hades's abode, breaking a taboo against eating underworld food, and so was condemned to remain there. Eventually a compromise was reached by which she spent half of each year underground – during which time the human world experienced winter – and the other six months in the upper air, when her return brought the spring.

The interior of this long barrow at Gavrinis, east of Carnac in Brittany, is aligned to the midsummer solstice. The precise significance is unknown, though the stones are thought to mark the graves of warriors. The spiral decor represents the journey of the soul, travelling through death to rebirth – an eventuality probably connected to the life-giving powers of the sun.

The abducted-goddess stories introduced a sexual element into the seasonal drama absent in the all-male myths mentioned earlier. This note was especially pronounced in the Sumerian legend of Inana and her lover Dumuzi, which described how Inana, the Queen of Heaven, descended to the underworld kingdom of her sinister sister Ereshkigal. At its seven gates, she was successively divested of all her robes and insignia of royalty; the formulaic way in which the disrobing was couched suggests strongly that it was re-enacted by her earthly worshippers in a seasonal ritual. Finally she was left naked and powerless in her dread sister's sway.

As in the case of Idun and Persephone, her disappearance had terrible consequences, though in her case the effect was on procreation; all love-making ceased on Earth. Only when she was rescued through the agency of Ea, god of water and of wisdom, did the generation of new life resume again. Later versions of the myth made it clear that she had gone to the underworld to rescue Dumuzi and that he also returned with her. The text ends: "May the dead rise and smell the incense".

At first sight, this story may seem to have little to do with the seasons, but the relevance is made clearer by a related tale from Syria about the rain god Baal (see page 50). For Baal too was swallowed by Death, and in his case it was his sister Anat who went to look for him. And when Death refused to give him up, she responded violently. In a ritual-sounding phrase, she "cut Death with a blade, winnowed him with a winnowing fan, parched him with fire, ground him with a millstone", and finally scattered him in the fields. In other words, she treated him like the harvested ears of corn, including the new planting. As a fertility goddess, she took Death itself and turned it into new life with the changing of the seasons.

Another seminal myth from the Middle East took the story one step further. The tale of Isis and Osiris was central to the religion of ancient Egypt. It told how the devoted couple – siblings as well as spouses – were brutally parted when their envious brother Seth killed and dismembered Osiris and scattered the fourteen parts of his body all over Egypt. Devotedly, Isis combed the land to find the fragments. One version of the myth then claimed she put them together and brought Osiris back to life; another, that she buried each one where she found it, bringing fertility to previously barren land. Her quest was symbolically re-enacted in periodic fertility rituals around Egypt, when it was specifically linked to the theme of renewed life and the cycle of the harvest. And, significantly, Osiris, who at first had been a god of vegetation and growing plants, in time also became the divinity of death and the afterlife. The connection had been made between the annual renewal of the crops and personal resurrection. It was one that was to resonate in many other religions.

For behind all these tales of dying or disappearing gods, an even older tradition lingered. This is a pattern of myth traced by scholars all across Oceania, Southeast Asia and the Americas. The story it told was of a shaping event long ago in the first ages when a supernatural being, whether god or spirit, was killed and then dismembered. Yet from this act of violence came new life, for seeds germinated and sprouted from the body of the deity – usually those of the peoples' principal food crop. And often this primeval action would be re-enacted in ceremony, with a sacrificial animal or sometimes even a human standing in for the slaughtered god. The ritual then becomes a remembrance of that original, cosmic sacrifice on which all subsequent life depended. Death melding into life, life into death – in the seasonal round, both were inextricably and eternally interconnected.

Deadly Festivals of Divine Worship

Spirits took human form in many mythologies; more rarely, humans might temporarily take on the attributes of gods, although very often at a high price to themselves.

One way the divine could manifest itself on Earth was in the person of a god-king, reigning as an intermediary for the heavenly powers (see pages 80–83); another, briefer revelation came in shamans' trances, when soul-voyaging mystics were temporarily possessed by the spirit of the divinity they set out to consult.

But stranger events still were in evidence in Mesoamerica. Among the Aztecs, a youth was selected annually to take on the persona of Tezcatlipoca, Smoking Mirror, a feared figure in the pantheon. For an entire year he stood in for the god, being feted and venerated by all. As the time of Tezcatlipoca's festival neared, the emperor visited him and he was given four wives, each the living representative of an important goddess.

Then came the fatal day when the god-surrogate had to mount the pyramid in Tenochtitlan, where priests were waiting to cut his heart out. His body parts were then cooked in a stew and served to the ruler and other dignitaries at a feast – next year's victim numbering among the diners.

In another, equally gory ritual, some Aztec warriors donned the skins of dead captives who had been sacrificially flayed and wore them in public, collecting alms and receiving homage, until the flesh had rotted away. The young men did so to impersonate and honour the fertility deity Xipe Totec, Our Lord the Flayed One and one of the four sons of Ometeotl (see page 15), during and after the agricultural festival of Tlacaxipeualiztli held each spring.

The symbolism was evidently that of agricultural renewal: just as the new maize emerges from the rotting husk around it and covers the body of the Earth again, so the Aztec warrior burst from the skin, "rejuvenated".

A statue of an Aztec warrior dressed in a sacrificial victim's skin to honour Xipe Totec during the agricultural spring festival.

The Great Goddess

The spirit of the seasons was only one aspect of the pervasive feminine principle in myth. So universal was the cult that some scholars have postulated the existence of a single Great Goddess, worshipped under different forms and different names around the world.

Among the earliest known works of art are the so-called Stone-Age Venuses. Carved from bone or stone, these small, crudely formed female images are almost unimaginably old, dating back as much as 25,000 years, a quarter of the time since *Homo sapiens* first emerged as a species. The surviving examples – about sixty in all – have been found at sites ranging from France to Siberia, and all show similar characteristics. At a time in the last Ice Age when food must have been scarce, they are markedly obese. And the fatness is concentrated on the breasts, thighs and buttocks – areas of the female body associated with sex and pregnancy. There seems little doubt that they celebrated fertility and reproduction.

Not to be confused with the Greek goddess of the same name, Artemis of Ephesus was a mother goddess from Asia Minor. The animal heads, bees and multitude of exposed, egg-like breasts reinforce the impression of a woman intended as the very personification of fecundity. The temple built in 550BC in her honour at Ephesus, where the original of this statue was housed, was one of the Seven Wonders of the ancient world. The figure may be influenced by the Anatolian figure of Cybele, who gave birth at Ephesus and constituted one of the many *Magnae Deae* or Great Goddesses acquired by Rome.

The image of the large woman had surprising longevity, too. The first examples were produced in the Old Stone Age. Yet sculptures dug up at the sites of the world's earliest towns – such as Catal Huyuk in modern Turkey and Mohenjo Daru in Pakistan's Indus Valley – recognizably celebrate the same bounteous female figure, and they date from almost 20,000 years later. The ubiquity of the symbolism has led some scholars to postulate the existence of a single deity, the Earth Mother, venerated across whole swathes of the early world.

The evidence for such a claim is necessarily scanty, though traces of similar beliefs survive in several far-flung mythologies. For example, the Andean peoples still retain the memory of their own Earth Mother, Pachamama, whose body was the Earth itself; she brought forth all that grows in it and took the dead to her breast upon burial. Even today, some people in the highland regions sacrifice llamas and guinea-pigs to her, along with beer, coca leaves and other plants. In the past, human victims were offered up as well.

The development of agriculture from about 10,000BC must inevitably have had a profound effect on any such cult. By the time the Earth

Ivory relief of the female goddess variously called Astarte or Ishtar, *c.*800BC. Among the Phoenicians, Canaanites and Mesopotamians she was the deity responsible for fertility. Ishtar was considered a patron of love and sex appeal, but in common with some other female deities she had dual attributes. Ishtar had a martial aspect, perhaps derived from the belief that her all-consuming passion resulted in the death of the objects of her affections.

Mother entered historical records, she was already a deity of the crops, and her worship was closely tied to the alternation of the seasons (see pages 59–60). Yet she had also retained her earlier connection with human and animal reproduction and motherhood, and had some quite unexpected attributes in addition.

The best known of these mother goddesses is probably the one venerated in the countries of the eastern Mediterranean. She went by different names in separate countries, and had varying aspects; but there is enough common ground in the myths about her to convince scholars that she was at bottom one and the same throughout. To the Sumerians she was Inana, to the Babylonians Ishtar, to the Phrygians of Anatolia Cybele, to the peoples of Syria and the Lebanon Astarte. In the Greek world, some of her attributes turned up in Artemis, others in Aphrodite and Demeter (see page 59). The Romans identified her with Gaia, Ceres and Tellus. Everywhere she was the Great Goddess, the Queen of Heaven, and she generated a special kind of religious awe.

In one of her aspects she inherited the maternal qualities of the old Earth Mothers. Seen in this light, the goddess was caring and gentle, satisfying a profound need for security and reassurance in a threatening world. This element in her worship eventually fed through into the Christian cult of the Virgin Mary, which the Church fathers traditionally looked on with suspicion, conscious of its ancient, pagan undertones; Mariolatry, as her excessive veneration became known, was frequently condemned.

Yet the need for a female goddess of healing and compassion was far from limited to the Levant. The Chinese had an equivalent figure in Guan Yin, goddess of mercy and still one of the most popular figures in the Daoist pantheon. Like Mary, she is often shown bearing a child in her arms, though her legend claims that, as an earthly princess, she faced execution rather than take a husband. Reborn as a Daoist Immortal, she demonstrated the depths of her charity by sacrificing her own eyes and hands for the father who had condemned her to death for refusing to marry.

63

Fairy Queens

Common in Western pantomime and folktale, fairy queens have their counterparts – maybe their inspiration – in Oriental mythology.

The Western tradition traces back to Morgan le Fay, an ambivalent character in the Arthurian romances, sometimes presented as a beautiful and seductive woman with healing powers and at others as a malevolent enchantress.

In their pantomime manifestation, however, fairy queens also take on some aspects of the Persian *peris* – exquisite, eternally beautiful female spirits who lived in treasure-filled underground palaces and were so refined that they could survive on scents alone. Their charms, and the wealth they could bring to the favoured, entered the Western imagination through the popular *Thousand and One Nights*.

Less familiar is the Chinese goddess Xi Wang Mu, who shared many of the *peris'* attributes. She lived in a mountain-top paradise attended by fairy maidens where she grew the life-prolonging Peaches of Immortality.

Xi Wang Mu in her heavenly garden paradise where the Peaches of Immortality grew that ripened only once every 6,000 years. Porcelain plate, 18th century.

Contrasting strongly with this spirit of self-sacrifice was another, less universally palatable part of the Near Eastern Great Goddess cult – its aggressive sexuality. Often the deities were linked with a male partner: Inana with Dumuzi, Cybele with Attis, Aphrodite with Adonis, Isis with Osiris. The couple's union was linked to the regeneration of the crops, and so had central importance to the well-being of the land. In some of the countries involved, this celestial act of coition seems to have been acted out in earthly rituals involving priestesses who served as sacred prostitutes and male hierophants who may in early times have been ritually killed after the love-making.

Other elements of the goddess's cult that troubled conservative opinion were the orgiastic rites through which adherents expressed their devotion. Priests of Cybele performed ecstatic dances in which they cut themselves with knives; they also castrated themselves in the goddess's honour. Our word "fanatic" comes from the Latin *fanatici*, literally, servants of the *fanum* or temple – a word used to describe priests of the Anatolian goddess Ma, who were similarly famous for their uncontrolled excesses.

Here too parallels can easily be found in other mythologies. The Scandinavian goddess Freya, still commemorated in the word "Friday", was famous for her promiscuity; it was said that she had slept with every member of the Norse pantheon. A celebrated tale described how she agreed to favour four dwarfs in order to obtain the Brisingamen – a magic necklace they had fashioned that symbolized the earth's fruitfulness.

Maybe the least predictable element in the cult of the Earth Mother was one that linked the goddess to death and resurrection. The connection seems to have come about through the burial of the dead in the earth, her own domain; by a process of comparison, it seemed logical to hope that she

A breastplate from the tomb of Tutankhamun, depicting the king in the form of the ruler of the underworld, Osiris, with whom every pharaoh was identified after death. He is protected by the "Mighty Ones", the twin female deities Nekhbet and Wadjet, one the vulture goddess of Upper Egypt and the other the cobra goddess of Lower Egypt. These were just two of many fierce rather than nurturing female protectors. From the Valley of the Kings, Thebes. c.1361–1352BC.

might bring them back to life, just as she regenerated the crops. So Persephone, the spirit of spring, spent half of each year in the underworld as Hades's consort; and in ancient Egypt too, the great goddess Isis was inseparably connected with Osiris, ruler of the kingdom of the dead,

Yet however unexpected the contrasts in the cult of the Near Eastern Great Goddess may seem, they can easily be matched in other parts of the world. Consider India, for example, where Lakshmi and Parvati, the gentle companions of the gods Vishnu and Shiva, rub shoulders with the terrifying Durga and the divine destroyer Kali, assassin of her own children and one of the great warrior-goddess figures of world mythology. As women, all these deities carry within them the source of life, while simultaneously possessing the means and the will to end it.

Yet in Indian popular religion, the most venerated goddess is none of these. Rather it is a more ancient figure who is honoured in humble shrines up and down the land. Hiding behind many names, the Grami Devi or local goddess is the village guardian who makes the crops grow — in other words the old fertility deity, worshipped now much as she must have been 10,000 years ago at the dawn of recorded time.

65

Tricksters and Troublemakers

Tricksters were the anti-heroes of the world's myths. Greedy, lecherous and endlessly self-seeking, they still won grudging admiration for their quick wits – and sometimes for their skill in triumphing against the odds.

In Freudian psychoanalysis, the mass of primitive instincts and antisocial energies that underlie the conscious mind go by the name of the id. In the world of myth, this untrammelled force, whose only object is the immediate satisfaction of selfish desire, showed up most directly in the shamelessly self-serving character of the tricksters. These experts in self-advancement appeared in cultures across the globe, universally loved by story-tellers seeking light relief for audiences sated with mythology's high dramas. In character they ranged from loveable rogues to thoroughly evil creatures who would stop at nothing, including rape and murder, to get their way. What united them all – and engrossed listeners worldwide – was their delight in their own cunning and their endless determination to get their way.

Despite their lowlife antics, tricksters frequently played a part in sacred mythology, and could themselves be gods (see also pages 32–33). Typically they occupied an intermediate position in the celestial hierarchy, sometimes serving, like the Greek Hermes or North America's Coyote, as messengers for the higher divinities. In many cases they took animal form. West African mythology had tales of Anansi the spider; Indian legend recounted the exploits of Hanuman the monkey general; the peoples of North America's Northwest Coast told legends of Raven; and in nineteenth-century United States and medieval Europe respectively, people enjoyed stories of Brer Rabbit and Reynard the Fox. Elsewhere they were often shapeshifters (see box, page 68) with the ability to take on the appearance of beast or human.

For all their wiliness, tricksters were by no means always clever; in fact their cupidity could easily turn them into dupes. In North America in particular, a whole category of tales described the trickster being too smart for his own good. A typical example was the tale of the sour acorns – a native delicacy. Coyote was told how to prepare it by soaking and pressing the nuts, but refused to believe that the recipe could be so simple. Only when his interlocutors, in exasperation, told him jokingly that the real method was to load them in a canoe and dump them in the river did he take them at their word – only to see the hoped-for treat float away out of reach downstream. Other buffoon tales had tricksters diving into ponds after the reflection of fruit hanging above their heads or setting fire to their own rear-ends in punishment for not having kept watch behind them.

The Importance of Wits

Another branch of the tradition delighted in showing the trickster outdone in the course of a ruse or else falling victim to his own trickery. In a Lakota story from the American Plains, Icktinike cheated Rabbit out of his furs, only to get his comeuppance when Rabbit responded by giving him a cowhide blanket made from skins that had also been used to make war drums. Whenever the drums were beaten, the blanket vibrated in sympathy, causing Icktinike to jerk so violently that he eventually broke his neck.

In Greek myth too, the wily Odysseus – a complex character whose trickster side was only one part of a multi-faceted nature – initially tried to avoid having to go to the siege of Troy by feigning madness. To convince the Greek leaders who had come for him that he was out of his head, he pretended not to recognize them and set about ploughing his fields crookedly, sowing salt instead

The medieval Reynard cycle was a popular series of moralistic fables using anthropomorphism as an effective way of making satirical social comments, mostly through the wiles of the hero fox. French manuscript illustration of an episode from the 14th-century romance *Reynard the Fox and Isengrin*, showing Reynard being chased by a farmer and his wife as he tries to seize a cockerel.

of seed in the furrows. But the hero Palamedes called his bluff by throwing Odysseus's own infant son in front of the plough. Instinctively the father reined in his team, inadvertently demonstrating that he was rational after all.

More typical, though, were the stories in which tricksters triumphed over great odds. In these tales they could take on some attributes of the mythic hero, often including an unusual birth (see page 87). What differentiated them was that they relied purely on quick wits to come off best, not on strength or courage. Usually, too, there was a comic aspect to the narratives, though also an element of cruelty absent from the version of the tales now often passed on as children's fables.

A typical example involved the Zulu trickster Hlakanyana and described the time he got caught by an ogre while trying to remove some dead game from the giant's traps. He persuaded his captor not to eat him there and then on the grounds that he would make an altogether tastier meal if taken home and cooked. So it came about that he found himself in a perilous situation – left alone in the ogre's kitchen in the care of the giant's old mother as she heated water in a cauldron to boil him for dinner.

Relying on his wits to save him, Hlakanyana volunteered to get into the pot, realizing the water must still be only lukewarm. He waited until it was as hot as he could stand, all the while pretending that it was still cool and quite unsuitable for cooking. The woman became puzzled. So Hlakanyana quickly offered to change places with her so she could see for herself.

Needless to say, he jammed the lid on the cauldron as soon as she stepped in and left her there to stew. Then, dressing up in her clothes, he proceeded to serve her to the ogre on his return. The giant found the meat so appetizing that he even called his brother in to share it. Only when they had finished did Hlakanyana reveal himself – and the horrible truth of their cannibal banquet.

Sometimes the gods themselves could be the victims of trickster cunning. A well-known Greek story described how the infant Hermes stole Apollo's cattle, putting bark shoes on them to prevent the deity from following their trail. A similar tale from Africa concerned Legba, the first man in the myths of the Fon of Dahomey. He stole yams from his divine father, but wore God's sandals to carry out the theft. He then produced the footwear and compared it to the prints in the yam patch to persuade the rest of newly created humankind that God had been guilty of robbing himself.

Sometimes tricksters used their ingenuity to more worthwhile ends, for in certain mythologies they played a role as culture heroes (see page 32). So Anansi the spider, who spent most of his long career doing nothing more worthwhile than fulfilling improbable boasts, began it all on an altogether more elevated note by spinning the entire world at the behest of the sky spirit. In India's epic *Ramayana*, Hanuman the monkey general found the hero Rama's lost-love Sita and also saved Rama's life in the final battle. His Chinese equivalent, Monkey, overcame innumerable obstacles to bring the Buddhist scriptures to the imperial court from India. And Maui, the great trickster of Oceanian tradition, not only persuaded the sun to lengthen the days so people had time to do their work but also dragged up from the ocean the North Island of New Zealand, which is still known as Maui's Fish in the Maori language to this day.

Magical Abilities to Transform

In myth's fluid world, animals and people could change places, and creatures of flesh and blood were not always what they seemed.

In early religion, most gods enjoyed the power to change shape at will. Unconstrained by physical limitations, they could imagine themselves into any form they chose. Greek Zeus came to Earth sometimes as a bull.

In later times, voluntary shapeshifting was mostly limited to tricksters and wizards; Celtic folklore in particular was full of such empowered characters. Less commonly, people could be forced to change their form involuntarily. The classic examples were werewolves of eastern Europe, but there were also were-jaguars in South America, while China had many foxes that took human shape.

All such tales presupposed a magic world beneath outer appearances in which the power of the imagination could overcome nature's ordinary laws.

The jaguar was the top predator of Central America's rainforest. Revered for its fierceness, it served many important functions in ritual transformation; the Olmec were-jaguar was said to derive from human-animal mating. Ceramic, 12th–14th century AD.

Taliesin and Elphin

In legend, wizards like the Welsh Taliesin inherited the ingenuity and magical powers of the trickster divinities.

A real-life Taliesin existed in the sixth century, but little is known of his life. By the time the *Book of Taliesin* was written 800 years later, much legendary material had gathered around his name. It was said that he became court bard to Prince Elphin, one of the local rulers who competed for favour at the court of great King Arthur. And the book also told how he came to his patron's rescue when the prince was imprisoned for rashly boasting that he had a more faithful wife and a more gifted bard than any other knight at the king's court.

As he lay in a dungeon, a suitor was sent to his palace to disprove the first claim by seducing his wife. But Taliesin's powers of clairvoyance were such that he foresaw what was planned. He persuaded a kitchen maid to stand in for the real princess, dressing her in royal robes. So when the ravisher cruelly sought to prove his conquest by cutting off one of the girl's fingers to take back to court, Elphin had little difficulty in showing that it was not his wife's. It was too fat and the nail was untrimmed; moreover, it bore traces of dough, which a princess would never have had cause to knead.

Thwarted in his first attempt to discredit his prisoner, Arthur next insisted on organizing a contest of bards. But Taliesin's powers were such that he magically reduced all his opponents to mumbling incoherence. Then, when his own turn came, he sang so sweetly that he burst the very chains that held his master captive. The king had no choice but to agree that Elphin had been right in both his boasts, and thereafter he treated both Elphin and Taliesin with nothing but the very greatest respect.

Yet in his cosmic role the trickster could equally well be a force for destruction. Following only his own self-interest, he could do harm as easily as good, and sometimes deliberately sowed dissension for no more reason than to satisfy a whim. So Coyote, according to the Maidu people, introduced suffering and death into the world simply out of boredom, because he found the world's original state of perfection insipid. In Micronesian legend, the trickster Olifat gave sharks teeth and scorpions stings simply for the fun of it. And in Aborigine tradition, the troublemaker Tjinimin was held responsible for having speared the Rainbow Snake in the Dreamtime. Writhing in its death-agonies, the gigantic serpent created the Australian landscape as it exists today, but also put out all the fires in the world. It was only through the efforts of the culture hero Kestrel that one charred stick was saved, and so the light and warmth people needed to survive were preserved.

Yet tricksters, in their mindless self-absorption, could do even worse, as Norse myth showed. For in the tales of the northern gods, it was the evil trickster Loki who engineered the death of Balder, god of light and joy. And it was he too who was destined to lead the frost-giants on Asgard at Ragnarok, so triggering nothing less than the end of the world.

69

Guardians of Hearth and Home

The domestic world had its own mythology and its own cast of spirit-helpers. Benign or troublesome, their goodwill had to be courted by householders who wanted to enjoy the security of a peaceful, well-ordered home.

Ever since humans first started living in permanent residences, they have felt a natural urge to seek protection for their homes. More than just shelters to keep out the elements, these were refuges for those who lived in them, offering havens of warmth and security in an otherwise threatening world.

The need became greater in the age of agriculture, as populations became more sedentary. Homesteads now could last a lifetime. In the country, peasant farmers and their families could attain a degree of self-sufficiency that meant they rarely had to stray far from their fields. In the spreading towns, walls and doors offered a sense of individual space and a modicum of privacy from the teeming throng.

To preserve home and family, householders naturally turned for help to the gods. But the great creator deities must have seemed too remote to aid in such intimate duties. Instead they looked for support to less forbidding presences. The household custodians of the spirit world for the most part had a down-to-earth, even comic aspect. Even when credited with divine powers, they were treated by their beneficiaries with the familiarity due to a family friend.

In many ways the earliest known example was typical. Bes, the domestic deity of ancient Egypt, was homely in every sense of the word. A bearded, long-haired dwarf with bandy legs, he was certainly no beauty. And he was approachable, too; his taste for such human pleasures as music, dancing and the company of children was enough to make him welcome round any hearth.

In fact he seems to have had his origins in Nubia to the south as a warrior god; when the soldierly Romans eventually adopted his cult, they revived his early aspect by dressing him in a military tunic. But for the Egyptians and the Greeks, who also took him up, his ridiculous appearance undercut any such martial pretensions. Instead, they chose to identify him with fertility. In Egypt he became a guardian of women in labour; while the Greeks, with ichyphallic directness, chose to portray him as a rampant satyr.

One way or another, his image was more widely reproduced than almost any other Egyptian god's, carved on doorposts, bedsteads, chairs and other furniture to ward off evil spirits. Bes was also thought to encourage fertility, protect children, drive away snakes, and generally bring good luck. In these attributes he effectively served as a prototype for all subsequent deities of the home.

The Roman Gods

Besides accepting Bes into their pantheon, the Romans had their own domestic deities in the *lares* and *penates* honoured in every home. Lar seems originally to have been a farm god, protecting the harvest on its way to market, but in time he accompanied the peasants into the cities and became identified with ancestors' spirits. The

Lar, Roman deity of the family, representing the home and the spirits of the dead. Most households had miniature shrines modelled on Roman temples which contained depictions of both the *lar* – the family's special deity – and the *penates*, or gods of the store cupboard. At mealtimes small portions of food would be offered to the latter to encourage them to ensure a regular supply of food. Small bronze statuette, 1st century AD.

Lar familiaris – family Lar – had his own honoured place in a cupboard shrine in every living room, where offerings would be left to win his favour.

The *penates* were guardian spirits of the store cupboard – *penus* in Latin – who, if properly treated, guaranteed that there would always be food on its shelves. They were usually thought of

as a pair. Families who did not want to go without took care to offer them a small portion of food at every meal and provided them with a salt-cellar for their convenience. They also had a sanctuary, in their case near the hearth, which was sacred to yet another protective deity, Vesta, the goddess of fire. A flame was always kept burning there in her honour; if by any mischance it went out, it had to be freshly struck from a fire-wheel rather than relit from an existing brand.

In many cultures the world over, houses are in themselves a sacred space, often shaped to mirror the order of the cosmos, or else oriented to serve a ritual purpose. The cliffside dwellings of Mali's Dogon people reflect myth in their structures, for their thatch-roofed granaries reproduce that of the Master of Pure Earth who descended from the sky on the fourth day of creation. Symbolic of a fertile female figure, the granary is divided within into eight storage spaces corresponding to the eight Dogon ancestors and the eight internal organs of the body.

Sanctified Homes

Domestic shrines of the Roman type were in fact an international phenomenon, and they have their successors today in the images of saints, bodhisattvas and Hindu deities that still adorn the

walls of millions of homes worldwide. In Japan, where Buddhism and the old Shinto faith comfortably co-exist, many homes to this day have a "god-shelf" lined with statuettes of holy figures chosen haphazardly from both faiths. In South America similar images have now largely replaced the *huacas* or sacred objects of pre-Christian times. Usually these took the form of roughly carved or oddly shaped stones, placed in niches or wrapped in cloth to provide spiritual protection; but in early days they sometimes included the mummified body of a dead ancestor, kept in a place of honour in the house and paraded publicly through the streets on the annual Feast of the Dead

A very different tradition survived in China, where a whole range of different domestic deities was charged with the supervision of every corner of the house. In keeping with the bureaucratic nature of the nation's pantheon, they took an intrusive interest in the behaviour of the families they were intended to protect. In particular, the Kitchen God served as a celestial Big Brother, charged by the Ruler of Heaven to take careful note of any misdeeds, from slovenly housekeeping to lack of deference to the aged. Once a year he travelled to the

celestial court to file a report on all he had seen. In practice, householders regarded this divine tale-telling light-heartedly; on the eve of his departure, it was traditional to offer the god alcohol to make him tipsy, or to bribe him with glutinous sweets in the hope that his lips would remain sealed.

Domestic Mischief

In European lands the old domestic deities were driven underground when Christianity replaced pagan beliefs, resurfacing in the form of household spirits. These godlings lacked the authority of

China's Kitchen God started life as a human with a very ungodly past. In fact he embodied repentance, for in his mortal aspect Zao Jun was a man named Jang who left his wife to marry his mistress. His behaviour did not go unpunished; the gods blinded and bankrupted him, and the mistress abandoned him. Homeless, he wandered the streets as a beggar. Then one day he smelled a delicious odour wafting from a house. He stopped to ask for food, and was invited inside. The noodles tasted delicious, but also familiar – and as soon as the lady of the house spoke, he realized chance had led him to the home of his former wife. Overcome by shame at the wrong he had done her, he threw himself into the fire and was burned to ashes. After his death, the gods took pity on him as a repentant sinner and made him the Kitchen God, responsible for overseeing the behaviour of the family – and never far from the hearth in any home. Kitchen god holding court, 19th-century print.

their fully divine predecessors; instead they tended – at least when riled – to behave more like mischievous poltergeists on the rampage. The Slav world was particularly rich in them; besides the *domovoi* who lived behind the stove and who was often thought of as the spirit of a dead ancestor, there were more malign beings associated with farmyard, barn and bathhouse, all of whom could cause serious trouble when nettled. Their cousins in western Europe included the German *kobold*, the French *lutin*, the Scandinavian *nis* and the Spanish *trasgu*, a red-robed dwarf who roamed houses at night, doing housework or breaking furniture as the mood took him.

One common feature of all these pesky spirits was that they were hard to get rid of, as a story told of their English counterpart, the boggart or brownie, relates. This tells of a farmer driven to distraction by the depredations of a particularly energetic boggart, who regularly spilled his milk, freed his cows and horses, banged his doors and broke his dishes.

Finally deciding he could take no more, he loaded his possessions on a wagon and was about to abandon his farm when a friend came up to ask what he was doing. He barely had time to start recounting his woes when a small, supernatural voice broke in from the top of the cart to explain, in a rustic accent, "Don't you know, we're flittin'". The boggart had decided to come too.

In the eastern Baltic lands a different tradition survived. It told of a thieving spirit who served the master of the house by bringing home stolen goods. In Finland this familiar was known as a *para* or "bearer" and often took the form of a cat. Usually it purloined nothing more valuable than dairy produce, grain or milk, which it carried in its mouth, though it might at times disgorge money.

Rather more spectacular was the Lithuanian *aitvaras*, a small flying dragon that resembled a cockerel when grounded but a fireball while airborne. It too specialized in petty larceny, though it was so regular in its depredations that it was thought of as a giver of great wealth – maybe a folk-memory of the treasure-guarding dragons of

Lithuania's *aitvaras* were said to cost a great deal to buy, their value deriving from the riches their owner could accumulate through their thievery. It was claimed that some people sold their souls to the Devil in order to acquire one.

ancient northern myth. Perhaps its greatest eccentricity was its diet, for it lived on omelettes – a taste all the more unexpected as the *aitvaras* itself was jestingly said to be bred from cock's eggs. Otherwise it had to be bought for a great price.

Such tales now belong firmly in the realm of folklore; they are told to entertain, and nobody is expected to take them seriously. In a world of security alarms and house and contents insurance, it may seem that the old need for reassurance as to the sanctity of the home is finally dead. Yet some traces of the old beliefs still remain; every time a family says grace before meals or sets up a wall-hanging saying "God Bless This House", they are unconsciously echoing a tradition of entreaty dating back at least 5,000 years.

73

SINUOUS AND ETERNAL SYMBOLS

Ancient in origin, serpents or dragons, often both, are found in most cultures worldwide, but their meanings and symbolism differ. The word "dragon" is derived from the Greek *drakon*, meaning a "large serpent", and this mythic, hybrid creature was in essence a snake-like, winged reptile. Dragons were frequently viewed as manifestations of primal energy – commonly depicted as fire-belchers in the West and water-bearers in the East. The Chinese thought the dragon kings lived underwater but could ascend to the skies to bring rains; very positive notions existed about dragons or *lung*, for it was believed they were strong sources of male energy or yang, whose presence was discernible in mighty clouds of vapour and violent thunderstorms. Such dragon kings were repositories of power, able to bestow blessings on those mortals deemed worthy – an attribute which made them the perfect imperial symbol. In Australia and Africa too, creation and life-giving water were strongly associated with serpents, whose meandering coilings were reminiscent of the endless movement of flowing streams.

The Aboriginal Rainbow Snake, for example, was an ancestral figure whose primeval tracks had been marked into the landscape since the Dreamtime; as too had those of Aido-Hwedo among West Africa's Fon people. But perhaps the greatest association of all was with dark forces. There persisted a widespread symbolic use of serpents as the embodiment of malificence. They perhaps owed their evil reputation to their preference for dark, subterranean places that people feared. In addition the serpent's shape inevitably suggested phallic associations that lent themselves to tales of desire and lust. Conversely, snakes' ability to slough their skins and emerge anew meant they were sometimes envied as adepts of rejuvenation. The contradictions perfectly encapsulated their ambiguous standing as objects simultaneously of attraction and repulsion.

Left: **The Hindu god Vishnu the preserver sits on the coiled serpent, Ananta-Shesha, which floated on the primordial ocean. Vishnu holds his usual attributes – a shell, mace, disc and lotus – and wears a sacrificial cord around his torso. As Kurma, the second of his ten incarnations, he supported the Earth during a flood with the aid of the great snake Vasuki. Cobras form a five-headed protective canopy, their hooded appearance reminiscent of the *nagas*, the snake servants of Varuna.**

Above left: Ancient Egyptians believed the universe depended on the sun surviving a nightly struggle against the forces of evil, represented by the serpent god of darkness and trickery, Apophis. This female cobra symbol or *uraeus*, rearing up as if defending the wearer, was part of the pharaonic regalia belonging to King Sesostris II, c.1847–1837BC.

Above: In Near Eastern tales, serpents often represented chaos and darkness, and were frequently confronted by heroes. Triumphs over monsters featured in northern myth too, in the exploits of such warriors as Siegfried and Beowulf. The negative Eastern image filtered into Christian use as the embodiment of pagan sin, and medieval art

frequently depicted saints undertaking the religiously symbolic feat of vanquishing terrifying dragons. In the process the slayer was often believed to acquire the attribute of fertility, and barren women frequented many saint's shrines. Ethiopian icon representing St George's dragon-slaying heroics, 18th century.

Below: Dragons in Japanese mythology reflected the influence of China, from where they were originally imported. They could alter their size at will, even becoming invisibly small, and often served as menacing foils for heroes to grapple – such as Susano's encounter with Yamata no Orochi. Detail from a 19th-century triptych by Sadahide.

Right: As a child, Herakles signalled his potential by strangling two snakes sent by the goddess Hera to kill him. Later, as a man, one of his Twelve Labours was to confront the many-headed watersnake known as the Hydra. When one head was severed two sprang up to replace it, making it very difficult to kill. Roman finger ring, 2nd century AD.

Left: In many African creation myths
the snake was considered the most
ancient of creatures, there from the
very beginning of time. The cosmic
serpent acted like a World Tree, linking
together the different levels of the
emergent universe with its coiled body.
Gold snake ornament from the Ivory
Coast, 19th century.

Right: Five-clawed Chinese imperial
dragon depicted among sky clouds
and guarding the flaming pearl, which
represents the sun and imperial treasure.
Silk robe of a eunuch from the court
of the Empress Dowager, 19th century.

Above: Twisting across a ridge in
southwestern Ohio, the Great Serpent
Mound is one of the most enigmatic
monuments of America's Adena culture,
which flourished from approximately
600 to 200BC. Archaeologists have
found no signs of graves or ritual objects
around it, giving them few clues as to its
intended purpose. Half a kilometre in
length from tip to tail, the gigantic figure
holds an oval shape in its mouth that
may represent an egg – a primordial
symbol associated around the world
with the origins of life – leading some
scholars to speculate that the snake
represented a creation deity.

GOD-KINGS AND SUPERMEN

Unlike creation and nature myths, which peopled the world with gods and spirits, hero-myths – tales about individuals of extraordinary strength, courage and achievement – put the human race firmly in centre focus. While in the great stories of the world's making gods often descended to Earth to live like men and women, here the roles were reversed: exceptional people took on something of the power and purposefulness of gods. Found around the world, these myths were most widespread in those cultures such as ancient Greece that stressed individual human potential.

The urge to identify with outstanding beings seems to be almost universal. So, it more surprisingly turns out, is the underlying pattern of their exploits. Reduced to its bare bones, this is a tale of preparation, departure and return. First comes an exceptional birth, often into difficult or dangerous circumstances, followed by a childhood rich in portents. In late adolescence the hero may face a test that proves his fitness to confront what lies ahead.

Then comes the central quest as the hero sets out to perform great things. This climactic action is followed by a homecoming that may be triumphant but is just as likely to be troubled, disturbing all the comfortable compromises reached by those who have been left behind. Then, at the last, a remarkable life will be capped by a memorable death, often in tragic circumstances.

Hero-myths are so potent in their appeal that their roots evidently lie deep within the archetypal recesses of the human consciousness. Yet in some cases they may also have had other, more direct sources. Many purported to tell the stories of mighty figures from the past, and in some cases – most memorably for the Toltec ruler Topiltzin and the heroes of the Trojan War (see pages 84–85) – these claims have been shown to have some basis in fact. One derivation of the myths may lie in pre-literate societies' historical memory.

Alongside the hero-myths, a parallel tradition existed of individuals credited with more-than-human powers. These were the god-kings, real-life rulers who were believed by their people to have attributes of divinity. Usually these revered beings served as a living link between their subjects and the celestial realm; when they died, they were often themselves worshipped as deities.

Above: A 19th-century effigy representing the Central African king Chibinda Ilunga, founder of a Luba-Chokwe dynasty and a revered mythological figure.

Opposite: Herakles, a son of Zeus and the greatest of Greek heroes. This Roman marble head is some 2,000 years old and is probably a copy of a Greek original from *c.*325BC. Herakles or Hercules was popular across the Greek and Roman world because of his strength and defiance in the face of death.

Divine Rulers

Before the heroes, there were the god-kings – rulers believed to have been sent from the divine realm who used their special connection to the deities to justify an earthly sway unquestioned by their subjects.

History's first recorded god-kings are still the best-known examples of the breed: the pharaohs of Egypt. They were the earthly embodiments of Horus, the god known to every Egyptian as the winner of an epic struggle with the troublemaker Seth. Just as Horus's victory brought order to the divine realm, so his fleshly representative on Egypt's throne, the "living Horus", was expected to bring peace and stability to the human world.

The divine lineage of the pharaohs was impeccable. They were sired by none other than Re, Egypt's supreme solar deity, himself. The mechanics of the process were spelled out in the mortuary texts of Hatshepsut, one of the few female sovereigns in the nation's long history. Perhaps because traditionalists looked askance at a woman's seizing power, she took care to record the details of her celestial siring for posterity.

Her inscriptions described how the great god, taking the form of the reigning ruler Tuthmose I, came to her mother while she lay sleeping in the palace, waking her with his divine fragrance. Desiring her, "his love passed into her limbs". Before he left, the god informed her that she would bear a

daughter who should be named Khenmatemen Hatshepsut, "She who Amun Embraces, Foremost of Women" – and so it duly came about.

As the representative of the gods on Earth, the pharaohs had to ensure *ma'at* or "harmony". As one text put it, "Re has placed the king on the earth of the living for ever and eternity to judge humanity and to placate the gods, to bring right to fruition and to annihilate wrong". Even though they might in practice delegate much of the responsibility to their priesthood, in principle the sovereigns alone could intercede for the people in the heavenly realm. And they spoke not just for Egypt but for the whole of humankind, for – again in theory – all other nations were regarded as subordinate to them; in the language of Egyptian diplomacy, the pharaoh did not negotiate with foreign powers but only received their tribute.

The Egyptian system was only one of many different forms of sacred kingship known from around the world, each different in its details and its emphasis. Yet some factors were common to most. The link to the gods, for example, could serve to unite societies by giving earthly governance the stamp of divine authority; fractiousness or dissent in such a

Bronze statue from *c.*664–525BC of Horus, the falcon-headed god of Egypt, making a divine offering. The kings of the Second Dynasty had represented their struggles in terms of the conflict between Horus and Seth for the throne of Horus's father, Osiris. Upper and Lower Egypt came to be associated with Seth and Horus respectively.

context verged on blasphemy. In a threatening world celestial connections provided reassurance for the ruler's subjects, who took comfort from the belief that their government, inspired by higher powers, could be counted on to do the will of the deities in the human sphere.

Descent from the Sun

Among those rulers who asserted divine lineage, the usual line of descent was from the sun. Just as the Egyptian monarchs looked to Re, so the emperors of Japan traced their origins back to the solar goddess Amaterasu, who reigned over the other deities of the Japanese pantheon on the High Plain of Heaven. Uniquely, they preserved their claim to divine ancestry well into the twentieth century; it was only after cataclysmic defeat in World War II that the then emperor, Hirohito, was persuaded to broadcast an assurance to the nation that he was not in fact a god.

The late-nineteenth-century reformers who sought to re-establish Japan as a great power had in fact deliberately emphasized the divinity of the imperial line as a way of bolstering national unity. They were not the first to use a solar connection for political ends to judge from the evidence about another famous line of god-kings, the Inca of Peru. Current knowledge suggests that Pachacuti, the ruler who raised the dynasty to its brief spell of greatness, made a conscious decision to identify his house's fortunes with the sun god Inti, up to then a relatively humble member of the Peruvian pantheon. Not only did he raise Inti to a position of pre-eminence in the celestial hierarchy; he also took every opportunity to stress the imperial link, constantly reiterating it in official pronouncements, adding new festivals to the sacred calendar and forcing worship of the god on conquered peoples.

There were obvious reasons why an autocrat should seek to link himself with the sun. It was not merely the most splendid object in the heavens, dazzling in its majesty and glory, but was also the light-bringer without whose rays life on Earth would wither. Even so, the solar model was by

Test of a King

The Alur people of Central Africa told a tale of a hero-king vindicated by the gods through the actions of a dumb animal.

Ojanga-Mbele was the founder of the Alur kingdom, but his rule was contested by fractious nobles who put up a rival candidate for the throne. The issue came to a head at the annual festival of Rubanga, the rain god. It was the custom each year to offer a cow to the god, and everyone accepted that the king was the only man who could carry out the sacrifice.

So Ojanga-Mbele suggested a trial. He and his rival should each instruct the cow to kneel down before them in homage. The pretender tried first, threatening and cajoling the beast, which obstinately refused to budge. Then Ojanga-Mbele stepped forward. As the priests and elders watched in amazement, it slowly lowered itself to the ground in an act of submission before him. The message from Rubanga was clear. Ojanga-Mbele was the true monarch, and from that time on all the Alur showed him reverence.

Faces peer from the stepped, 12th-century ruins of Bayon at Angkor Thom in modern-day Cambodia. The Khmer emperors who commissioned these temple complexes were influenced by Javanese Shailendra dynasty notions of kingship. These developed into the concept of the *devaraja*, a god-king in whom temporal and spiritual authority were fused. Jayavarman II, for example, identified himself with Shiva. Another ruling idea was the temple mountain, a complex – akin to those found in Mesoamerica – which stood on an elevation and in which the king's divinity might be considered to dwell. Such monuments, still awe-inspiring, were considered the embodiments of the king and his world, intended to last well beyond his death.

no means the only one adopted in such circumstances. Rulers of the early Mesopotamian city-states, for example, often sought to aggrandize their dynasties by stressing their links to the local divinity, claiming not to be gods themselves like the pharaohs but to rule as delegates for the heavenly powers. At Ur, the relationship was symbolized each New Year's Day when the king ascended the city's highest ziggurat (stepped pyramid) to be joined in a symbolic marriage to a priestess representing Inana, the fertility goddess.

Incest and the Royal Bloodline

A fact of life in some dynasties which traced their origins to the gods, incest also featured in a significant number of the hero myths – though the consequences for the perpetrators were often dire.

The pharaohs of ancient Egypt occasionally married their own sisters; later, under the Ptolemies, the practice even became the norm. In Peru, too, it was the custom for the ruling Inca to marry a sister on his accession to the throne. The practice emphasized the gap between the divine king and his subjects, to whom incest was forbidden, and also maintained the genetic exclusivity of the ruling line.

In the hero tales too, incest occasionally occurs as a way to concentrate the bloodline; in the Norse *Volsung Saga*, for instance, Signy tricks her own twin brother Sigmund into sleeping with her, for she knows that only a full-blooded Volsung can avenge the terrible wrong done to her family.

Several celebrated heroes were themselves the products of incestuous unions, underscoring their distance from the norms governing the rest of society. So the Greek heroes Castor and Adonis were both born to their own grandfathers.

Yet incest was rarely tolerated in the heroes themselves. South America's Chibcha people told of a ruler named Hunsahua who fell in love with his sister. When she bore a son, the couple were hounded from their lands and were eventually turned to stone.

Mythical Lineages

Another approach was taken in certain eastern lands with a long recorded past and a firmly established tradition of dynastic power. The historical bias of these cultures led them to trace their kingship back beyond the limits of the known into mythical realms that directly linked the current monarch to the gods. Along the way the dynastic line would typically be ornamented by a series of culture heroes (see pages 32–33) – rulers with semi-divine powers who bestowed on their subjects the various blessings of civilized life. The moral was clear enough: people who owed so much to their ruling line would be foolish to show its present representative anything less than absolute respect.

Persia was a case in point. Its great epic, the *Shahnameh* or "Book of Kings", traced creation back to Allah (it was composed in Muslim times), but then delved into ancient legend to recount the first monarchs. The earliest king, it claimed, was Keyumars, who introduced food and clothing to humankind. He was succeeded by Hushang, to whom people were indebted for metalworking, irrigation and fire. Their succcessors passed on the secret of writing, taught humankind how to spin and weave, and promulgated the different social classes. In their wake came a line of monarchs who, though themselves subject to the limitations of mortality, were nonetheless superhuman in their attributes and powers.

But the historicist tradition was most firmly rooted in China – fittingly so, for no other country had a longer record of genuine monarchical rule. Even today scholars trace the nation's history to the Shang dynasty, traditionally stated to have come to power in 1766BC. But the early histories went back even further to an earlier line of kings, the Xia, whose founder, Yu the Great, fought dragons and had shapeshifting powers – and Yu also had predecessors. There was Yao, in whose reign ten suns appeared in the sky, and before him Huang Di, the Yellow Emperor, who gave humankind the boat and the wheel. Even further back came such shadowy figures as the bird-headed Shen Nong, who introduced agriculture, and serpent-bodied Fu Xi, giver of cookery and fishing. The inheritors of these ancient, shamanistic divinities never ceased to venerate their forebears; and, illuminated by their divine aura, they continued to rule a great empire for more than three and a half millennia until the last emperor was finally driven from power as recently as 1912.

History into Myth

In pre-literate societies, myths were the memory of entire peoples. As though by a process of Chinese whispers, the deeds of real-life kings and warriors might be magnified down the generations until they blossomed into archetypal tales of wonder.

For many years, historians of ancient Mexico were confused by references in Aztec sources to the god Quetzalcoatl. Generally portrayed as a feathered serpent, he was one of the leading deities of the Mesoamerican pantheon. But some references gathered after the Spanish conquest seemed to sit oddly with his divine persona. They described him in human form, tall with a white skin and a flowing beard. And they spoke of his defeat and exile; making his way to the Gulf of Mexico, he sadly took leave of his followers and sailed away, supposedly on a raft of serpents to the mythical land of Tlapallan.

Such a drama of rejection and withdrawal seemed oddly human for a god whose activities were otherwise on a cosmic scale, and so scholars now believe it to have been. For the Aztecs cherished memories of an earlier people, the Toltecs, whose gods they inherited and whose spiritual successors they felt themselves to be. All that is known of Toltec history comes down in distorted form through Aztec hearsay. And that, in essence, is what the story of Quetzalcoatl's exile is now thought to represent.

The confusion seems to have come about when a Toltec ruler named Topiltzin adopted the cause of Quetzalcoatl, even adding the god's name as an honorific extension to his own royal title. The decision was a political one, for the worship

The divine snake-bird figure of Quetzalcoatl from the *Borgia Codex*, probably produced in the late 15th century and now named after Cardinal Borgia who acquired it.

of this gentle deity set Topiltzin-Quetzalcoatl and his followers against the votaries of a rival divinity, Tezcatlipoca, whose cult was one of blood and human sacrifice. For a time, Topiltzin was in the ascendant, and in the folk memory his rule was later feted as a golden age. But at the time it ended in disaster and disgrace; the myths spoke of him falling for a ruse of his enemy, who got him drunk and caused him to commit a terrible offence, violating his own sister. For the crime he was expelled, and he set off to the east; some believe that his destination was Chichen Itza in the Yucatan peninsula, whose ruins today show a striking architectural similarity to Toltec styles.

In an additional twist to the tale, the Aztecs hoped that Topiltzin would return again one day to usher in a new time of peace. So when the Spanish conquistadors – bearded white men, sailing in from the east – arrived, many people, including the Aztec ruler himself, believed they might indeed be Topiltzin-Quetzalcoatl and his retinue come back, an illusion that ended in bitter deception when Cortes and his men brought only fire and the sword.

In its inextricable mingling of fact and legend, the story of Topiltzin is a case study of the way in which real events can take on new form in the distorting mirror of myth. Sometimes scholarship and archaeology can combine to untangle the web, as they did for Topiltzin. But other examples remain obscure, creating enduringly fascinating mysteries. Historians still argue, for instance, about the legends of Thunupa. This Andean culture hero – again bearded, again white – was said to have brought knowledge of cotton-weaving and the cultivation of fruit and vegetables to the region. Fiercely puritanical, he opposed promiscuity and strong drink. Eventually he was put to death by a local chief and his body was transported miraculously across Lake Titicaca on a reed boat. Some versions maintained that he carried a Cross – a detail that priests latched upon to claim him as one of Christ's apostles, perhaps St Thomas or St Bartholomew.

Uncertainty also surrounds Britain's King Arthur, mentioned in Dark Age chronicles as a native leader resisting Saxon invaders in the sixth century. Whether he was a Welsh or British chief or a professional soldier in command of a body of Roman-trained mercenaries – in fact, whether he ever truly existed – remains hotly debated. The one sure thing is that if he did his life can have borne little resemblance to the dream of chivalry elaborated around his name centuries later by the poets and romancers of the Middle Ages.

Much speculation goes unchecked, but there have been other cases in which legend has been shown to have some real historical roots. It was once common to dismiss Greek accounts of the siege of Troy as pure invention, the fantasies of poets. Then Heinrich Schliemann dug up the mound of Hisarlik, near the southern mouth of the Dardanelles in modern-day Turkey, and showed that such a city had indeed existed and contained treasures. Subsequent excavations turned up a short-lived layer that showed evidence both of unusually elaborate facilities for storing food and of destruction by fire – a combination that sits well with the Homeric story. It now seems likely that, however much it may have been elaborated in the telling, the siege nonetheless had some basis in fact.

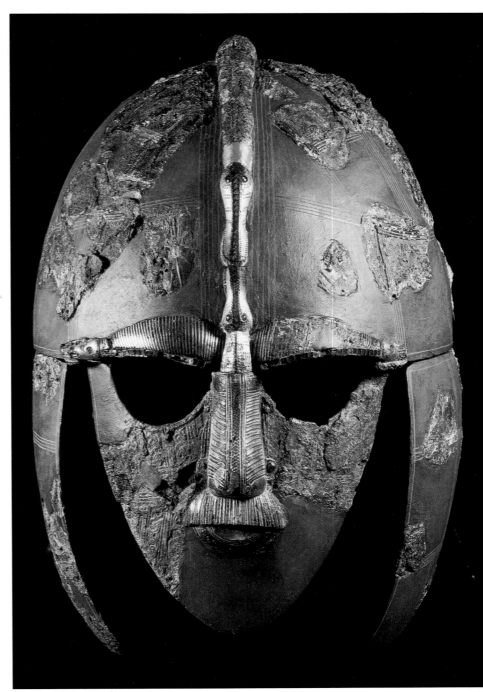

Pre-7th-century Saxon warrior's mask-helmet found at Sutton Hoo in Suffolk, eastern England. It is made principally of iron, though the stylized dragon forming the nose and mouth is of gilt-bronze, with red eyes of garnet. For a warrior society such as the Saxon one, tales of heroic figures of the past were an important part of their culture; indeed most cultures draw upon history for inspiring feats to emulate, irrespective of the accuracy of the information.

The Call to Glory

Every hero was different, but even so their stories fit a recognizable pattern. First came an unusual birth, then a childhood rich in portents – all leading up to the fateful moment when the individual had to accept his fore-ordained destiny.

Everyone knows the qualities of heroes. They are strong, resolute, resourceful and brave. Above all, they are effective. Untroubled by self-doubt, they face seemingly impossible challenges and do what is necessary to overcome them.

Mythic heroes were also mostly male, for reasons that are not hard to understand. Set primarily in the human world, the tales necessarily reflected the societies that produced them, which for the most part limited the role of women. There is no shortage of powerful women in mythology, but usually they are goddesses operating on the divine plane where social constraints did not apply.

However vigorous and single-minded they might have been, heroes rarely lacked faults. Sometimes they might have a physical weakness – Achilles's heel, for example (see page 89) – or could labour under a debilitating curse, like that which periodically rendered Ulster's Celtic heroes powerless. More often they displayed mental flaws: Odysseus's deviousness, Herakles's occasional lapses of judgement, Roland's pride. Even so, their general intentions were necessarily always good – otherwise they would not have been heroes.

Yet the protagonists of the major myth cycles were linked by more than mere lists of qualities.

Their lives conformed to a recognizable pattern that has been explored by many writers, notably the American Joseph Campbell. In broad outline this was a tale of departure, accomplishment and return. Some call took them away from the familiar world on a journey in which they confronted terrible dangers and monsters. At its end they attained some noble goal and then made their way home, often to the discomfort of those they had left behind. Their deaths were often sad or tragic.

Yet the similarities run deeper than that quick sketch might suggest, stretching even to relatively minor details. A comparison of the life stories of half a dozen heroes from different parts of the world quickly shows up unexpected echoes and points of contact.

Extraordinary Infants

The likenesses start from the very beginning, at the moment of the heroes' conception or birth, which usually took place under unusual circumstances. The child might be born by Caesarean section, like Persia's Rustam, or be the result of a virgin birth like Vainamoinen, the hero of Finland's national epic the *Kalevala*. Or else the mother may have been deceived as to the true identity of the father – the future King Arthur, for instance, was conceived when Uther Pendragon, King of the Britons, fell in love with Igraine, wife of the Duke of Cornwall, and persuaded the magician Merlin to give him the appearance of her absent husband. A similar theme cropped up with the Greek hero Herakles, whose begettor was the god Zeus, who had taken the form of his mother's betrothed. To enjoy his clandestine pleasures all the more, the king of the gods extended the night of passion to three times its normal length.

A 15th-century Turkoman-style Persian miniature from Firdowsi's epic masterpiece the *Shahnameh* depicting Rustam killing a dragon during the second of his seven trials. Rustam personifies the idealized human hero in Persian culture, vanquishing all opponents, whether natural or supernatural, and confronting any manner of predicament in order to restore order and well-being.

Abandoned Children

A classic element of the hero myth was exposure to danger soon after birth, and the child's subsequent adoption by strangers.

This pattern was common in Greek myth, where the infant is often condemned to die by a father or grandfather who feared being supplanted. So Perseus was locked with his mother Danae in a chest and cast out to sea, only to be saved when the vessel fetched ashore on an Aegean island. Oedipus had a spike driven through his feet and was abandoned on Mount Cithaeron outside Thebes, but was rescued by a herdsman. Paris was similarly left to die on a mountainside and was saved by a she-bear who suckled him.

In Roman myth, Romulus and Remus were rescued by a wolf. The Persians told tales of the hero Zal, who was found as a baby by the legendary bird called the Simurgh and raised with her own young.

Probably the best-known example of all is the Biblical hero Moses, set on the Nile in a basket of bulrushes. Yet even this account has a close parallel in Indian legend, where Karna, one of the heroes of the Hindu epic the *Mahabharata*, was floated by his mother in a rush container on the River Acva. Like Moses, Karna was rescued, though in his case by a humble charioteer rather than by the pharaoh's own daughter.

A mosaic from Britain of the she-wolf rescuing Rome's founders, the abandoned twins Romulus and Remus.

Alternatively, the mother might become pregnant through a dream. The Celtic hero Cuchulainn traced his origins in that way to the god Lugh. Gesar of Ling, the focus of Tibet's best-known epic, was born in an egg that emerged from his mother's head after a lord had ridden up to her in her sleep and given her nectar to drink, telling her she would bear a child who would liberate her country. Oddest of all was the genesis of China's warrior champion Nezha. After his mother had carried him for a painful forty-two months, she fancied one night that a Daoist priest had entered her room as she dozed, thrusting a bundle into her arms. She awoke to find herself in labour and bore a round ball of flesh that rolled across the floor. Her husband rushed in and chopped the monstrosity in half with his sword, and Nezha calmly stepped out, already able to stand on his own feet.

However bizarre, the first appearance of a future hero was merely a portent of things to come. Often the infant showed by some special sign or token that he was destined for great things.

A common episode for heroes is a confrontation with a giant. Here, the Japanese hero of the Minamoto clan, Yorimitsu, is accompanied by his loyal retainers in just such a deadly encounter. One of the best-known of his aides was Kintaro (centre, below), who had acquired fame as a child due to his enormous strength and wisdom, acquired partly by having been brought up with wild animals as his friends and playmates.

The infant Achilles provided a variation on the theme. His mother, Thetis, was a goddess who had been forced to marry a human. Insulted by the match, she plunged all her babies into flames, in order, she claimed, to burn off whatever was mortal in them. In all she lost six children in this way. But her husband prevented her from killing the seventh – Achilles. In a last-ditch attempt to protect her son from the human lot, Thetis dipped him in the River Styx, whose waters conveyed immortality. It was only because she forgot also to moisten the heel by which she had held him that he was burdened with his notorious weak spot.

The threat could also be more immediate. The infant Herakles strangled two snakes sent by the jealous goddess Hera to kill him and his twin brother as they slept. And Gesar of Ling survived various attempts on his life by a courtier who sensed the presence of a future rival. Buried alive, he emerged unscathed; attacked by demon birds, he shot them down with his toy bow and arrows.

Later in childhood, the hero may start to reveal his true nature by precocious acts of daring. At age twelve, Cuchulainn killed the fierce watchdog of Culann the smith and offered to take its place until a new one could be found, winning his name – which means "Hound of Culann" – in the process. Theseus, of Minotaur fame, attacked a lionskin left by Herakles on a visit to his father, when all the other children of his age had run off screaming, mistaking it for the real thing.

The Stepping Stones to Greatness
Finally, as the youth approached manhood, he often found himself confronted by some sort of test. This trial of strength stood at the threshold of

Nezha, for instance, brought with him a bracelet and a piece of red silk that in time turned out to have magical powers. He was also exceptionally big, a common mark of distinction – Rustam was said to have required the milk of ten wet-nurses.

Despite such hints of incipient greatness, the world into which the future hero emerged was rarely waiting to welcome him with open arms. A surprising number of hero-tales featured the motif of children who survived against the wishes of those around them (see box, page 87).

89

The Triumph of Wolfdietrich

The Germanic tale of Wolfdietrich is a classic hero legend, involving childhood rejection, dragon-slaying, a period of exile and a triumphal return.

Wolfdietrich was the son of Hugdietrich, Emperor of Constantinople, and the beautiful Hildeburg. But their marriage was a secret one, for Hildeburg's father Walgund would permit no suitors, and the child was born while Hugdietrich was away at the wars. One time when Hildeburg had to leave the baby outside the tower to prevent her parents from discovering him, he disappeared, only to be found days later in the forest nearby playing with wolf cubs. From that incident he won his name.

In time Walgund did learn of the marriage and was reconciled to it. Wolfdietrich grew up proud and strong, in every way a suitable heir to the imperial throne. But in Constantinople a faction refused to accept him, spreading the rumour that he was not Hugdietrich's child. When the old emperor died, this group succeeded in driving Wolfdietrich from the city, setting his two younger brothers on the throne in his stead.

From then on, Wolfdietrich's life was devoted to redeeming his honour and regaining his rightful inheritance. He had to suffer many trials on the way. At one point he fell into the hands of a hideous witch, Rauch-Else, who took the form of a she-bear; but when he consented unwillingly to marry her, she turned into a beautiful princess with whom he lived happily for many years. Then he sought to enlist the aid of Ortnit, king of the Lombards, in his cause, only to find that his intended ally had been killed by a fearsome dragon. In true hero fashion, Wolfdietrich insisted on confronting the beast, and succeeded in killing it and its brood with the aid of a magic shirt of invulnerability and a sword whose blade had been tempered in dragon's blood.

Eventually, after many trials, he returned to Constantinople and triumphed over his enemies. Then he returned to Lombardy to be crowned Holy Roman Emperor – perhaps a historical memory of Theodoric the Great, a real ruler who seized power in Italy in the sixth century AD.

his time of greatness. The challenge served as a watershed; beyond it, he left behind all hope of a normal life, opting instead for the heroic route with all its attendant risks and dangers.

One such feat – maybe the most familiar one – was the pulling of a sword from a stone. The best-known example involved the future King Arthur. At the time when Excalibur appeared in the marketplace of the town where he lived, bearing the legend "Whoever draws this sword from this stone is the rightful-born king of all England", Arthur was only a lowly squire. But, forgetting his master's sword one day when it was needed for a tournament, the youth took a tug on the hilt – and the blade yielded easily, even though many older and seemingly stronger knights had failed to shift it. When he repeated the feat three more times, his future stood plain as England's predestined ruler.

In fact the Excalibur story was a relatively late addition to the Arthurian canon, and it was probably preceded by a Norse tale of the twin children of Volsung, King of the Huns. Interestingly, this also included elements of the troublemaker-at-the-wedding motif familiar from folktales such as "Sleeping Beauty". At the marriage-feast of his daughter, Signy, a stranger – in fact the god Odin – strode into the hall and thrust a sword deep into the beam supporting the roof, saying that it would belong to whoever could remove it. Signy's brother Sigmund did so, thereby humiliating his brother-in-law, who had tried and failed. And so the tragedy of the *Volsung Saga* swung into motion; in time it led to the family's destruction.

A similar story was told of Theseus, though in his case he had to lift a giant boulder to retrieve a sword and sandals his father had left to test his mettle. He then had to make his way to Athens to establish his true identity, deliberately choosing a dangerous path that exposed him to a series of challenges, fighting brigands and monsters. Such serial trials of strength, often dubbed "labours" in reference to the Labours of Herakles, were also a feature of Persian legend, cropping up in the career of the young Rustam as well as in that of another celebrated hero of the day, Isfandiyar.

Two of the main Arthurian figures were Gawain and Lancelot. Gawain was the nephew of the supernatural queen Morgan le Fay; Lancelot was also of royal birth, but had been abducted as a child and raised by the Lady of the Lake. This 15th-century image is an interpretation of one of the quasi-supernatural adventures found in *Le Livre de Messire Lancelot du Lac.*

At other times the trial could take the form of a contest the hero had to win if he was to embark on the path intended for him. So Gesar had to triumph in a horse race against all-comers to establish his claim to the kingdom of Ling – and did so despite the fact that his mount looked to be the sorriest in the chase. Or the hero's ingenuity may be put to the test. Menelik, the legendary founder of the kingdom of Ethiopia, was the illegitimate son of the great Solomon, but had never seen his father. When he travelled to Jerusalem to settle the paternity question, the ruler tried but failed to confuse him. Refusing to pay obeisance to an impostor masquerading as the king, he wandered the palace until he established his claim for good by instantly falling to his knees before his true parent.

And so, with the crucial challenge behind him, the hero stood ready at last to meet his destiny. Sometimes the change was apparent for all to see: Gesar on his broken-down dray became a shining knight on a matchless steed, and Menelik returned home to Ethiopia riding on clouds of glory. As often, though, the transformation was purely internal. The hero now knew the task that lay ahead; it was time to confront it with determination and singleness of purpose.

91

The Epic Quest

At the heart of most classic myths lay a quest. The hero had to leave the security of home for a world of dangers in order to achieve some great goal. He came back changed by the experience – and not always the happier for the memorable deeds he had performed.

Several writers have pointed out that the hero quest dramatizes the pattern of ordinary life, when children on the threshold of adulthood must quit the bosom of the family to make their own way. No doubt that familiar background helps explain the universal appeal of the theme; everyone can identify with the young adventurers on their outward passage. Yet in story it is only in simple folk- or fairytales that the protagonists merely seek the normal goals of love or money, typically in the form of a handsome prince or princess or a pot of gold. In the myths, the object of the seekers' strivings was altogether more complex.

Sometimes the target was dictated by necessity. Two of the best-known quest sagas took place in the wake of the Trojan War. In the *Odyssey*, the victorious Greek commander Odysseus – Ulysses in Romanized form – only sought to return home, but his voyage became an epic of endurance. In the *Aeneid* the eponymous Aeneas, a prince of the defeated Trojan royal house, had to find a new base for himself and his followers, journeying ultimately to Italy and becoming the founding father of the Roman people.

Accomplishing a Set Task

Other classical myths described the carrying out of a task; one of the odder features of the formula was that this was usually set by an enemy, thereby helping explain the great difficulty and danger attached to it. So Jason was sent to fetch the Golden Fleece by a fearful monarch who had heard from an oracle that the young man would eventually kill him. King Polydectes dispatched Perseus to bring back the Gorgon's head because he wanted the son out of the way in order to seduce the mother.

In the Mesopotamian *Epic of Gilgamesh*, written down as early as 1600BC, there were actually two fully fledged quests: one to kill the forest monster Huwawa, the other a more philosophical search for the secret of immortality. Sometimes the task attempted was purely personal, like Rama's search for his abducted wife Sita, which forms the backbone of India's great epic, the *Ramayana*. Or it could be for the benefit of society as a whole,

The Mystic Origins of the Grail

No quest legend is better known than the search for the Holy Grail. But the early history of the sacred vessel is altogether less familiar.

According to medieval legend, the Grail was carved from a single precious stone that fell to Earth at the time that Lucifer was cast out of Heaven. After many ages, the holy cup came into the hands of Joseph of Arimathea, who offered it to Jesus to use at the Last Supper. Later Joseph caught drops of the Saviour's blood in it at the Crucifixion.

From that time on the Grail had extraordinary healing powers. Not only could it cure sickness; it could also slow down the process of ageing, so those who guarded it could live for centuries. These miraculous properties helped sustain Joseph through persecution in the Holy Land, and later when he made his way first to Rome and then to an unspecified location in the south of France.

There he established a corps of a dozen grail-keepers, modelled on Jesus's own apostles. All were expected to live immaculate lives, and when one secretly sinned a terrible famine in the surrounding lands published the fact. To identify the evil-doer, Joseph made a table with twelve seats. Eleven of the guards sat down without mishap, but when the miscreant tried to join them, he was swallowed up. Henceforth that place was known as the Siege Perilous; only knights of pure virtue could sit there unscathed.

In one popular version of the legend, Joseph eventually brought the Grail to England, where it was preserved on the summit of Glastonbury Tor in the West Country. An alternative telling entrusts it to the care of a knight called Titurel, who was instructed by an angel to look for it on the summit of an otherwise unknown peak called Montsalvatch, thought to lie in Spain. Climbing to the summit, he was granted a vision of the sacred vessel and built a temple to house it with the aid of a band of companions who became known as the Templars – an actual medieval order, in reality dedicated to protecting the Temple in Jerusalem.

When the building was complete, the Grail appeared mystically within it, descending to the altar amid the singing of angelic choirs. Titurel himself then guarded it for several hundred years before passing on the charge to his son Amfortas.

Glastonbury Tor, Somerset, England. The hill – a prominent local landmark – is said to be where the Holy Grail, used in the Last Supper, lies buried.

93

as in Chinese legend when the monk Xuanzang and the Monkey King set off to bring the Buddhist scriptures back to their homeland.

Two of the greatest quest myths involved a hunt for an imprecisely defined object whose exact significance is still a matter of debate. By the high Middle Ages the Holy Grail, sought high and low by King Arthur's knights, had a pedigree in legend as the vessel Christ drank from at the Last Supper (see box, page 93). But Celtic specialists now think it may have started life in the earliest versions of the story as either a cornucopia producing endless supplies of food and drink or else as a vessel containing the waters of rejuvenation.

In the Chinese tale *The Journey to the West*, a monkey with special powers and a human body accompanied the monk Xuanzang on an epic journey to India to bring back the Buddhist scriptures. En route they encountered Pigsy and Brother Sand, and the four overcame 80 perils, including this fight against a female demon. Woodcut, 17th century.

Even more mysterious was the *sampo*, a bone of contention between the main characters of the *Kalevala*. The exact nature of this wonderful object, which lay concealed within a mountain producing endless wealth, was never actually made clear, and scholars still argue over it to this day. The word means "pillar", leading some commentators to think it was a wooden idol; others interpret it as a magical mill bringing forth an endless supply of salt, grain and money. Whatever the truth may have been, it guaranteed prosperity for its possessors, and the hero Vainamoinen organized an expedition to snatch it.

Most of the action in the stories was supplied by the ordeals that the seeker had to overcome on his way to fulfilling his goal. Sometimes, as in the case of the Twelve Labours of Herakles, these were in effect the quest itself; the Greek hero had to accomplish them in penance for the blood-guilt he had incurred by killing his own wife and children in a fit of divinely inspired madness.

Menelaus's battle with Hector, Troy's warrior hero, is depicted on a vase, *c.*610BC. The *Iliad*, Homer's poem about the Trojan War and its aftermath, describes the conflict between the Greeks and the city-state of Troy (called Ilion or Ilium in ancient times). The story began with the birth of Paris, who was abandoned by his father, Troy's King Priam. Having been welcomed back into the fold years later, Paris attended a wedding between the mortal Peleus and the sea-nymph Thetis, at which Zeus appointed Paris to judge which of three goddesses, Athene, Hera or Aphrodite, was the fairest. He opted for Aphrodite, thereby earning as a reward the gift of the world's most beautiful woman – Helen, wife of Menelaus, King of Sparta. But his decision incurred the everlasting enmity of the other two goddesses and the stage was thus set for an epic war.

Yet the trial-quest was not just limited to classical mythology. Another example came from the Buganda people of East Africa. They told how the first man, Kintu, had to perform a series of apparently impossible tasks – eating enough food for 100 people at a sitting; cutting firewood from rock; filling a large pot with water not from any lake, river, pond or well – in order to claim the daughter of the King of Heaven as his wife. He succeeded against the odds and went on to found the Bugandan royal line.

Sometimes the hero had preliminary tasks to accomplish before he could embark on the principal part of his enterprise. Rama had to find where his lost Sita was being held, a feat he accomplished with the aid of the monkey hero Hanuman; Perseus needed to obtain a magical cap, sandals and satchel before he could set out to confront Medusa. In another African tale, the young prince Djabe Sisse, searching for the lost city of Wagadu, first had to learn the language of animals and then seek the information he required from a lizard, a jackal and a buzzard in turn, each creature older than the one before. Then he had to feed the buzzard for ten days to give it the strength to bring back the magic war-drum, stolen by *djinns*, that alone could reveal the secret of the city.

Again, it is the Grail legend that contains perhaps the most hauntingly ambiguous of all such episodes. This occurs when the seeker Percival finally locates the Grail-castle in the middle of a barren wilderness, finding it in the possession of the mysteriously named Fisher King. A melancholy air hung over the place and its ruler, who was evidently sorely afflicted by an old wound. That night at dinner a strange procession passed through the great hall; maidens brought in an array of mystical objects including a branched candlestick and a bleeding lance as well as the Grail itself. Percival was too polite to enquire of his host the meaning of the spectacle. It was only the next morning, when he awoke to find all doors barred to him, that he learned that the entire court was under a curse that could only have been lifted by his asking the question he had not put. Five years were to pass before he got the chance to undo the harm he did by his apparent lack of curiosity that night.

A Hero's Helpers

Although heroes in fairytales might often set off on their own to achieve great things, their equivalents in the more elaborate hero-myths regularly called on companions to help them in their enterprises. Odysseus and Aeneas had their respective bands

95

of followers from the Trojan War. Jason invited warriors from all over Greece to accompany him to the Black Sea in search of the Golden Fleece; in all fifty-six were chosen, among them Herakles and the minstrel Orpheus. And Herakles himself gathered war-bands to help him on a couple of his labours; the Athenian hero Theseus and Achilles's father Peleus both accompanied him on the raid to snatch the Amazon queen Hippolyte's girdle.

Sometimes the assistants could be altogether less predictable in their nature. Gilgamesh could kill Huwawa only with the aid of Enkidu, a gigantic wild man who became his boon companion

over time. Rama's aides in the search for Sita included an army of monkeys provided by the monkey-king Sugriva. And in the tale of the quest for the Buddhist scriptures, Xuanzang not merely had the help of Sugriva's Chinese equivalent but also of two most unlikely sidekicks: the monstrous Pigsy, condemned to bear a pig's head on a human body, and another fallen celestial official called Brother Sand, who had previously eked out a living by stealing from passing travellers.

Alongside human fellowship, the heroes also often had the benefit of divine assistance. Monkey in the Chinese tale could count on the encouragement of Guan Yin, goddess of mercy, while Rama won the backing of the great god Shiva by raising an image in his honour. In the classical myths, the gods were fully fledged participants in the action, helping or hindering the questor as the inclination took them. Herakles was plagued throughout his life by the hostility of Hera, who despised him for

Desperate to rescue Sita, Rama (blue, at centre left), with the help of his monkey and bear allies, begins the attack on Lanka, the demon citadel where she was held captive. The god Hanuman and the monkey-king Sugriva had sent an army to serve Rama; in fact Hanuman himself played a crucial role in Lanka's destruction. A 17th-century manuscript from Rajasthan.

Two Disparate Hunts for Boar

Sometimes separate mythologies handle identical themes, revealing significant cultural differences in the treatment. So both Greek and Celtic legend told the tale of an epic pursuit of a monstrous boar.

In the Greek version, the district of Calydon north of the Gulf of Corinth was plagued by a beast sent by Artemis as a punishment when the local king, Oeneus, omitted to sacrifice to her. Many of Greece's greatest champions answered the king's invitation to hunt down the creature, which was causing chaos. It was finally brought down by Atalanta, one of Greece's few girl heroes. The coup de grace was delivered by Oeneus's son, Meleager.

For the Greek myth-makers, the greatest interest lay in the sequel to the hunt. Meleager, smitten by Atalanta, awarded her the pelt as a trophy, outraging his two uncles, who felt that it should have been kept in the family. In his anger, Meleager killed both, initiating a tragedy that led to his death and to the suicides of his wife and mother.

The Welsh tale of the hunting of Twrch Trwyth was recorded in the *Mabinogion* and the spirit is altogether more convoluted and comic. It describes how King Arthur and his men hunted down the boar of that name – actually a king transformed as punishment for his sins – in a gruelling epic chase through Ireland, Wales and Cornwall, in which dozens of people died. While the simpler Greek tale retains an element of realism, this Celtic version delights in exaggeration and culminates not in a killing but the removal of a razor, comb and scissors caught between the beast's ears.

Celtic boar made of bronze and dating from the 1st century BC.

being her husband Zeus's illegitimate son; many of Odysseus's misfortunes on the journey back from Troy were occasioned because he raised the wrath of the sea-god Poseidon by killing his son, the giant Polyphemus. On the other hand, Perseus could never have carried out his mission to kill Medusa without the aid of Athene, who gave him the burnished shield in which he saw her reflected image, so escaping being turned to stone. The same goddess also sped Jason on his way, giving him a bough from her oracle at Dodona that gave the power of speech to his vessel, the *Argos*.

In contrast to the goddesses, mortal women in this largely masculine world for the most part played a passive role. The protagonists often met, and sometimes fell in love with, beautiful maidens; but everlasting happiness was to be the preserve of fairytales. In the mythic quests, dalliance was more likely to be treated as a distraction. The hero might rescue a princess from a terrible fate, chained to a rock awaiting a sea monster, as Perseus did with Andromeda and Herakles with Hesione; but then he would move on to other pre-occupations, leaving the damsel behind.

In the classical myths at least, there was little chivalry in the heroes' treatment of women. Sometimes they cruelly abandoned them, as Theseus left Ariadne on Naxos, even though she had helped save him from the Minotaur. The results of the neglect could even be fatal; forsaken by Aeneas, Carthage's queen Dido stabbed herself to death on a funeral pyre. And even in the *Ramayana*, when Rama finally succeeded in reclaiming his kidnapped wife, he treated her not with courtesy but with contempt, suspecting her of committing infidelities with her abductor in his

Mounts Befitting Heroes

Heroes' relationships with their human companions were often troubled, but the bond that tied them to their horses more than withstood the test of time.

The equine link spanned many ages and cultures. In Tibet, Gesar of Ling won his kingdom by defeating all-comers astride his beloved mount Kyang Go Karkar. Arab tradition spoke of al-Borak, "Lightning", the human-faced, milk-white mare that carried the prophet Muhammad from Earth to the Seventh Heaven. The Persian hero Rustam's Rakhsh was so sharp-sighted that it was said to be able to see an ant's footprint on a black cloak two leagues away at night.

Norse mythology honoured the god Odin's eight-legged horse Sleipnir, which could cross land or sea, while the Germanic hero Siegfried was inseparable from Grani, a descendant of Sleipnir's that he originally chose by driving a whole herd into a raging river and seeing which had the stamina to cross.

Celebrated steeds from the medieval epics included Bayard, given by Charlemagne to the sons of Aymon, which could extend its size if all four wished to ride it at the same time, and El Cid's Bavieca, which survived him for two-and-a-half years without ever allowing another rider in the saddle.

The real-life model for some of the stallions of legend was Bucephalus, the inseparable companion of the Greek conqueror Alexander the Great. His biographers claimed that in adolescence Alexander revealed his heroic mettle by taming the stallion when no one else could. He did so by a combination of courage and astuteness, noting that the spirited young animal regularly shied away from its own shadow – and then taking care to approach it from the shaded side.

Persia's hero Rustam had a marvellous horse in Rakhsh. In this illustrated *Shahnameh*, c.1435, Rustam is shown catching his mount. He was said to be seeking not just strength and courage but understanding in the steed.

---

absence. Like Dido, Sita had to fling herself onto a pyre to show her love – though in her case she was rescued from the flames by divine intervention.

The Lesson of Experience

Driven on by an all-consuming purposefulness that could overcome any obstacle, the successful hero would finally attain his goal – but sometimes the moment of fulfilment was not all that he originally had dreamed. For every Percival and Galahad, who got to see the Holy Grail in all its glory, there was a Lancelot, barred at the door of the chapel because he was judged unworthy of the final consummation. Exhausted in mind and body by his long sufferings, Odysseus finally arrived back at his longed-for Ithaca asleep, to be cast senseless onto the beach by the Phoenician sailors who had carried him on the last stage of the journey. As for

Gilgamesh, he travelled to the ends of the Earth and beyond in his pursuit of immortality only to learn that his quest was in vain. Challenged to stay awake for a week, he found he could not even conquer sleep, let alone death, and had to set off homewards a sadder but wiser man.

Yet there were successful conclusions too. With the aid of the enchantress Medea – a significant exception to the passive-woman norm – Jason won the Golden Fleece and escaped homewards. After more than eighty separate adventures en route, Xuanzang and his companions acquired the prize of the holy scriptures from the Tathagata Buddha in person. In addition, the band were rewarded with the power of flight, greatly speeding up the return journey. Their homecoming too was an unclouded triumph, for they were feted by the Chinese emperor himself. While Xuanzang read from the holy writings to the assembled court,

he and his companions levitated, to the amazement of onlookers. They travelled on all the way up to the Buddha himself, who rewarded them all suitably. Xuanzang and the Monkey King received the ultimate accolade of becoming Buddhas.

Yet here too their experience was hardly typical. More often the heroes came back to a world that found their presence uncomfortable or threatening, menacing all the adjustments that had been made in their absence. Perseus arrived to find Polydectes still pestering his mother, but took a memorable revenge; with the king and his coterie gathered at a banquet, Perseus announced that he had brought the desired trophy. Then, removing the Gorgon's head from a satchel, he displayed it to the revellers, turning them to stone.

Jason had an even sourer welcome, returning to find that his parents had been murdered by his uncle, King Pelias. In his case, Medea effected a requital by persuading the ruler to plunge into a boiling cauldron that supposedly had the power to rejuvenate; in fact he died horribly. Odysseus's homecoming turned into a bloodbath when he and his son Telemachus slaughtered the ranks of suitors who had taken over his palace, hoping in his absence to win his wife Penelope's hand.

Again, the atmosphere of myth in this respect was markedly different from that of the happily-ever-after world of fairytale. Almost the best that the returning hero could expect was to be able to cultivate the wisdom won from hard experience in peace. Once more Gilgamesh turned out to be a trailblazer; reconciled however unwillingly to his own mortality, he returned to his home in Uruk and spent his latter years as king in beautifying the city. Rebuffed in his quest for divine status, he decided instead to make the best he could of the human world.

99

The Death of Heroes

Nothing became heroes so much as the manner of their going. Whether struck down while battling impossible odds or else carried off mysteriously, perhaps to join the gods, they left an afterglow that in time came to form a crucial part of their legend.

Heroes did not die easily; something special was required to overcome their exceptional strength and vigour. Sometimes it might be the hostility of the gods. In Greek myth, Bellerophon angered Zeus by flying the winged horse Pegasus towards Olympus; flung to Earth, he ended his days lame and blind, shunning human company. A similar fate awaited Jason after he broke his vows to his wife Medea. Dogged by divine disfavour, he wandered as a beggar from city to city, finally finding his way to Corinth, where the hulk of the *Argos* lay rotting. As he sat ruefully in its shadow, meditating on changed fortunes, the prow fell off, killing him.

Sometimes the divinities preferred to drive their victim mad. Attis, who spurned the love of the Phrygian fertility goddess Cybele, was dealt such a fate, castrating himself in a frenzy and bleeding to death. His cult survived in Rome, where priests of Attis practised ecstatic self-mutilation at a festival on 22 March each year, burying the severed organs in the ground to symbolize earth's regeneration.

When the agents of death were human, the odds had to be very great to explain a hero's frailty in succumbing. In the medieval Charlemagne cycle, Roland held off an entire Moorish army with his outnumbered rearguard before blowing a final blast on his horn and passing away. In Roman legend, Horatius Cocles held the bridge that led into Rome against Etruscan invaders until its supports were cut away and he fell, fully armed, to his death in the river below. Blind and chained, the Biblical Samson used his strength to bring down the temple roof on himself and the Philistines.

Northern myth laid special stress on courageous death, which supplied the measure of a warrior's worth. Before battles, Viking chieftains would order bards to sing the lays of heroes like Bothvar Bjarki, who fell along with eleven other

The death of Roland at Roncesvalles, from a 14th-century manuscript. A distraught Charlemagne weeps over the bloody body of his beloved nephew. A headstrong nature made Roland a contributor to his own demise.

Resurrected Kings

The legend of the ruler who will come back to protect his people from beyond the grave has a resonance that echoes around the world.

In Celtic tradition the "once and future king" is Arthur, who sleeps with his warriors under a hill and will return to re-establish the rule of the ancient Britons. Similar stories are told on the European mainland of Charlemagne, first of the Holy Roman Emperors, and of one of his great successors, Frederick Barbarossa, said to rest in the Kyffhauser Mountains in the Thuringia region of Germany. One version of the myth has him sitting at a marble board growing a beard; when it is long enough to encircle the table three times, the time for his re-emergence will have come.

Yet the motif is not limited to Europe. In the Hindu *Puranas* – ancient Sanskrit texts – King Mucukunda sleeps in a cave until summoned by Krishna. The Armenian hero Meher waits with his horse in a cavern, though he will not emerge again until the end of the world. Native Andean peoples put their hopes of salvation from their colonial masters in the reappearance of Atahualpa, the last Inca ruler. Such beliefs touch a deep millenarian strain that finds a religious equivalent in many faiths' belief in a Saviour's long-delayed return.

The African city-state of Ife was founded by Oranyan, who was ready to rise from the dead to protect the citizens when imperilled. Brass plaque of a royal figure, 16th century.

bodyguards of King Hrolf Kraki, a real-life ruler of Denmark in the sixth century. Another role model was Ragnar Lodbrok, remembered with pride for going to his death laughing (see box, page 103).

Unusually for the largely masculine world of hero myths, Norse women could match their menfolk in meeting their ends proudly. After sacrificing her sons to destroy her husband, Signy in the *Volsung Saga* walked into the flames of his burning hall, saying she had no wish to go on living. Queen Brynhild stabbed herself to death in order to be buried with her lover Sigurd, even though she, through jealousy, had engineered his death.

Sometimes heroes were brought down for no fault of their own but simply through the treachery of those about them. The Persian champion Rustam was unvanquished in battle, but was undone by the machinations of one of his relatives. Mounted on his faithful steed Rakhsh, he fell into a sword-lined pit prepared by his half-brother. Pierced by the blades, he still found the strength to climb far enough up its side to shoot down the traitor before falling back to die.

Death through betrayal was particularly common in legends of outlaw heroes, as two tales from different parts of the world illustrated. England's

Robin Hood went to an abbey to be bled for a sickness, only to find himself under attack when he was weak from loss of blood. Although like Rustam he killed his attacker, he was by that time mortally wounded, with just enough strength left to fire an arrow from the abbey window; with his dying breath he told his companions to bury him where it fell. In China Guan Yu, a great fighter for justice, was taken alive in an ambush and was offered his life if he would change sides. When he refused, he and his son were executed side by side. He subsequently attained a kind of immortality, revered as a god of war.

A distinctive feature of some myths was the point of vulnerability that made an otherwise invincible warrior mortal. In Germanic myth a similar tale to that of Achilles (see page 89) was told of Siegfried, who sought to protect himself from all wounds by bathing in dragon's blood; but a leaf fell between his shoulders, leaving an unmoistened spot that proved his downfall. From the Swahili-speaking peoples of East Africa came the tale of Liongo, a mighty warrior who could be killed only by a copper nail driven into his navel. He too fell victim to family treachery when his own son struck him down in his one weak spot.

Another element in the Liongo story has parallels in other parts of the world. Legend claimed that in his dying agony he staggered into sight of the nearby town of Shaka and put an arrow to his bow to fire at its walls. At that point he fell to his knees and died. But rigor mortis set in, and for three days no one dared venture out of the gates, fearing that he was still alive. The tale recalls that

of the Spanish hero El Cid, whose corpse was strapped to his horse to lead a final assault on his Moorish foes. And there are echoes, too, of the demise of the Irish warrior Cuchulainn, who strapped himself to a rock when he realized he had been fatally wounded. Again, no one dared approach the corpse for three days; it was only when the war goddess Badb landed on his shoulder in the shape of a crow and he did not stir that his enemies accepted he was dead.

Yet perhaps the most moving of all such deaths were the ambiguous ones, in which the champion simply disappeared. Persian monarch Kay Khusrow vanished into a snowstorm as his companions watched, while in one version of his legend, King Arthur was carried off across a lake into the mist on a barque bearing three queens (though another tradition suggests that he never died at all – see page 101).

There is a hint of divine apotheosis in all these tales that in some is more clearly spelled out. The dying Herakles, for example, was spirited away from his own funeral pyre in a hail of thunderbolts, sent by Zeus to summon him to join the gods. And Jainism's great teacher, Mahavira, was said to have been carried up to Heaven at the close of his ministry before an audience of the world's rulers. Feeling his end nigh, he summoned them to his presence and preached for seven days. At the appointed time he mounted a throne and the lights of the universe were dimmed. His audience fell asleep, and when they woke he was gone, carried off to Heaven. So, across very different traditions, the archetypes of the hero tradition find common ground.

Mahavira, born a member of the Hindu warrior caste, delivers his first sermon atop a dais inside his *samavasarana*, a circular structure of linked tiers created by the gods as an audience hall. The *tirthankara* or teacher was the 24th incarnation in the current cycle of celestial time, as understood by followers of the Jain religion.

Laughing in the Face of Death

One of the most celebrated hero's deaths was that of the Viking champion Ragnar Lodbrok, whose fearlessness was put to the supreme test in a pit filled with deadly snakes.

A familiar figure in Northern epics, Ragnar Lodbrok is thought to have been modelled on a real-life raider of the eighth century. In the tales, he was a fearless warrior who mounted the Danish throne at the age of fifteen and married the lowly ward of a peasant couple only to find out later that her true parents were the Germanic heroes Siegfried and Brynhild. He rescued another of his four wives from a castle entirely entwined in the coils of a huge dragon. The name Lodbrok or "Leatherbreeches" comes from the oxhide armour he is said to have worn for that exploit.

He is probably best known, though, for the manner of his death, which occurred after a raid across the North Sea to England. Captured by Ella, king of Northumbria, he was condemned to die in a pit of adders. At first he was shielded by a magic shirt given to him by his mother, but when this was removed he had no protection from the snakes' venom. Accepting his fate with equanimity, he bellowed forth a death-song proclaiming that he went to his end laughing.

Even so, he was ferociously avenged. His sons later captured Ella and disembowelled him by opening up his back and internal organs to form the image of a spread eagle.

CONFRONTING THE FINAL MYSTERY

If myths helped people in past times to come to terms with the big questions of human existence, there were none larger for them to answer than those raised by death's inescapable presence. Why did all living things have to die? What happened to people once they had passed away? Did they simply fade into nothingness, or could they expect something more? If so, what? More than mere curiosity was involved in resolving these conundrums; the answers had powerful implications for the way in which people lived their lives. After all, it was convictions about the afterlife that inspired the building of Egypt's pyramids and China's imperial tombs. And similar concerns served in less spectacular fashion to mould the hopes, aspirations and habits shaping untold millions of individual destinies.

Below: Lanterns floating on Motoyasu River in Hiroshima during the Buddhist ceremony of *bon*, held each August to honour the souls of the dead.

More surprisingly, perhaps, the answers provided were often quite similar, even across distant cultures. Many peoples in very different parts of the world chose to explain death's intrusion as the result of a mistake, or else as a punishment for human wrong-doing. Sometimes it was seen as part of a larger cycle, like the passing of the seasons or the crops' rise and fall.

Most groups came to the conclusion that there must be something beyond death, though there were various conflicting views of what it might be. Yet, once again, there was also much common ground in the details provided. All around the world, for example, people held that individuals denied the proper funerary rites would wander the Earth as restless ghosts.

Allied to this notion was the conviction, shared once again across cultures, that the deceased's soul embarked on a trek for which it had to be equipped. Even fine points of the necessary baggage could crop up repeatedly: in ancient Greece as in imperial China and South America, people put coins into graves to pay the tolls demanded on the soul's voyage to its final home.

And, in later times, there were marked similarities too in the tales that people told about the lands of the dead. Whether recounting epic quests by living heroes or terrifying one another with tales of ghosts returning from beyond the grave, they mined a seam of primal doubts and fears that ran deep into the archetypal unconscious and that are still as real as ever to this day.

Opposite: At one time Africa's Kota people's dead were left unburied in the forest and a reliquary figure, *mbulu ngulu*, such as this was laid alongside. Wood with copper and brass, Gabon, 19th century.

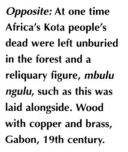

105

How Death Came into the World

People around the globe saw death as a cruel imposition, difficult to square with notions of a well-ordered universe. Some tried to explain its existence as a mistake, others as a punishment; but a third group sought to present it as a hidden boon.

Eager to protect the reputation of their gods, some peoples in Africa, Australasia and South America were even unwilling to accept that the divinities had any responsibility at all for human mortality. Instead they blamed people's deaths in general, and particularly sudden or unexpected ones, on the malice of sorcerers. One story from Angola addressed the point by having a hunter capture Death in revenge for taking his brother. But Death disclaimed all blame for the deed; and to prove his point, he took the man to the Land of the Dead to see for himself. Death paraded the newly deceased as witnesses. Some had died from hostile magic, others through their own folly. People, Death pointed out, had only themselves to blame; they should hold each other accountable, not the gods.

A Terrible Mistake

Another popular scenario saw the existence of death as simply a terrible mistake. In this view, the creator originally intended some quite different

Stairway to Heaven

A myth of the Wintu people of California's Pacific coast told how an act of spite by the trickster figure Coyote brought death to the worlds of both animals and humankind.

When the creator spirit Olelbis determined to create the human world, he intended to link it to Heaven by a stone staircase. At its top he planned to set two fountains – one of purification and the other for rejuvenation; people would merely have to climb the steps and drink from them to regain their youth. He entrusted the task of building the great ramp to two sibling spirits who took the form of buzzards. Happily they set to work.

But then along came Coyote – an impish trickster who loved to cause trouble. Seeing the pair so hard at work, he made up his mind to distract them. So he set about planting doubts in their mind about the worth of what they were doing.

What was the staircase for, he asked. Would people really want to spend their time going up and down, endlessly restarting their lives? Would it not be better for them simply to be born, live and then die? "Joy at birth and grief at death are better," he claimed, "for these mean love."

Coyote was never less than persuasive, and the brothers soon found themselves losing heart for their task. Eventually they gave up, and then in disgust pulled down what they had already built. Coyote was now alarmed, for he had secretly hoped to skip up to Heaven himself before the link was cut. In terror at the prospect of his own death, he made himself wings from flower petals. But when he tried to fly he fell to earth. And Olelbis, looking down from on high, decreed that he must die, just as all men and women would from that time on, condemned to their fate by Coyote's own weasel words.

arrangement, but something happened to upset his plans along the way. A popular story in many parts of Africa told how the founding father sent a chameleon to give humans the happy news that they would live forever. But the lizard dawdled on the way, so irritating the deity that he sent a second messenger with a dispatch contradicting the first. And this one – a speedy gecko – carried out the mission with lethal efficiency, arriving first with the news that humans must die. And so it has been ever since.

Sometimes the death-by-misadventure theme was linked with the notion of the casting-off of dead skin. Noting how snakes apparently renewed themselves by sloughing off their old coats, some myth-makers maintained that people had once had a similar ability. But always in the stories something went wrong. In one African version a serpent waylaid the messenger carrying the new skins, thus usurping a privilege intended by the gods for humans. In an Australian telling, children destroyed the new skins before their parents could put them on, thereby introducing mortality to the world.

Another group of stories insisted that death was at first only a temporary arrangement that, through some mischance, became fixed for all time. When, in a myth of the Huchnom people of California, the creator Taikomol buried the first man, he intended to bring him back to life the following morning. But when the corpse reappeared, the smell of putrescence was so bad that the rest of the tribe felt sick. Seeing their disgust, Taikomol abandoned the idea of resuscitating the dead.

Then there was the persistent notion of a debate over death that the wrong side won. In North America the devil's advocate was often the trickster Coyote, who used his wiles to persuade

people against their better judgement to accept their mortal lot (see box, pages 106–107). In Maori myth, the creator god Tane came to blows with the evil Whiro, and even though Tane won the ensuing conflict, Whiro subsequently sent death and disease to plague humankind.

A Suitable Punishment

The idea of death as a punishment was just as widespread, and sometimes the offence for which it was inflicted was trivial in the extreme. The Luba of the Congo, for example, claimed that God and humankind originally lived together, but the humans proved such noisy, troublesome neighbours that they were expelled to Earth, where they were ever after exposed to disease and death.

Alternatively, death could be inflicted on the world for the misdeeds of a single individual. In these cases, the blame was disproportionately often cast on a woman. Many mythologies had their own versions of the Greek Pandora's Box fable, in which misplaced female curiosity led to untold evils being unleashed into the world.

So Australian Aborigines recounted a legend with echoes of the Garden of Eden story, in which the first people were expressly forbidden to go near a certain hollow tree in which bees were hiving. The men obeyed, but one greedy woman was so eager to get at the honey that she chopped at the tree with an axe. Out flew Death in the form of a terrible bat, spreading mortality at the merest touch of its wings. And a well-known African myth described the tragic effect of the forgetfulness of Nambi, the wife of the legendary founder of the Bugandan royal line. When the couple were descending from Heaven to people the Earth, they were given specific instructions to hurry on their way. But halfway down Nambi realized that she had left behind the grain to feed their

For the Chinese, notions of both life and death were highly bureaucratic. Lifespans were alloted by civil servants working for the Ruler of Heaven. Once completed, the soul went to the realm of death ruled by Yen Lo Wang. This kingdom of the dead had ten separate hells, each for a particular type of sinner and governed by a Yen appointee. Yen Lo Wang, Ming-dynasty porcelain.

108

The Portentous Raven

Feared in many cultures as a harbinger of death and war, the raven was also grudgingly admired for its well-honed survival skills. In North America, Raven was a culture hero, but for the most part the bird had a sinister reputation as an augur of doom, just as it did in Edgar Allen Poe's eponymous poem.

The Celts associated it with the war goddesses Badb and the Morrigan, both of whom took raven form to hover over battlefields. In Norse legend, Odin used two ravens as his spies, scouring the world daily to bring back word of all they had seen and heard. To the Arabs the bird was Abu Zajir, the Father of Omens; seeing one flying to the left meant bad luck. In German folklore, a raven flying over a house could presage a death.

Yet an alternative tradition saw positive connotations, sometimes

in the very same traits that gave the bird a bad name elsewhere. The ancient Persians associated ravens with battlefields too, but linked them with Verethragna, their warrior god of victory. As a result, owning a raven's bone or feather was enough to give a fighter semi-divine powers.

A raven at the Tower of London. One legend states it will stand as long as the birds remain. The tale probably had its origins in stories of the Welsh hero Bran (literally "Raven"), whose head is said to be buried within its precincts.

chickens and insisted on going back. As a result, Death caught up with them, and his presence has been inescapable ever since.

A Necessary End

Other peoples took a more philosophical tack, seeking to present death, for all its evident terrors, as a necessary part of the larger picture, essential to the community's well-being. Some chose simply to see it as a rest for the weary; the Dogon of Mali, for instance, claimed their first ancestor begged for a release from the miseries of old age.

For others it was an ecological necessity in face of rising population levels. The Caraja people of the Amazon basin region maintained that the first humans lived in the underworld, but it became hopelessly congested since no one ever died. So people made their way to the Earth's surface, where they found enough living space but also mortality. In Persian mythology, the hero-king Yima tried to cope with a burgeoning population

by magically increasing Earth's size; but even his efforts could not cope with the problem, and after three successful attempts, the spirit of evil sent Ice Age winters that killed off most forms of life.

Implicit in such tales is a sense of a common good transcending the interests of the individual. Cosmic order, they suggest, may require personal sacrifice of an ultimate kind. Yet such an insight offered cold comfort to anyone facing up to their own impending extinction or that of loved ones. There was more consolation in the thought that, though the self might be temporarily erased by death, all was not lost.

Following such ideas through, one school of thought would develop the concept of rebirth – the re-emergence of the soul in a new form, as an actor might reappear in a different role on a stage. Another postulated an awakening to new life, but in another world to this one. Between them, these two arguments would open the way to the world's great religions. The mystery of death remained, but thanks to them its sting became less sharp.

109

The Soul's Journey

All around the world, people believed that after death the soul embarked on a voyage. One aim of funerary rites was to provide the equipment it would need along the way.

Native American myths spoke of villages of the dead approached along tracks very similar to those the soul had known when it was alive. In Egypt it took the route passed each evening after sunset by Amun-Re as he journeyed through the twelve caverns of the underworld. Each one was guarded by monstrous, animal-headed creatures; to negotiate them successfully the deceased needed to know the spells contained in the Book of the Dead, a copy of which went with them to the tomb.

A Chinese tradition spoke of seven ordeals on the soul's journey to reincarnation. First it had to confront demons, who would beat it mercilessly unless bribed with money provided at the funeral.

Then it passed into a judgement hall, where it was weighed as in the Egyptian tradition (see pages 112–113). Souls not burdened with guilt could pass through, but others again risked falling into the hands of demons. Next it had to run the gauntlet of hounds – dogs were often linked with the land of the dead – trained to sniff out wrongdoers. If it survived this ordeal, it came to a magic glass providing a glimpse of what lay in store in the next incarnation. After passing a vantage point from which it could take a last look back at the life it was leaving behind, it had to negotiate a narrow bridge spanning a terrible abyss. On the other side lay the final ordeal: the Wheel of the Law, from

Grave Goods

From the earliest times, people felt an urge to bury clothing, food, tools and sometimes treasure with the dead.

The custom of putting things in graves goes back a long way. Far into the Stone Age, individuals were buried alongside utensils and animal bones; one grave excavated in modern-day Iraq was so rich in pollen that archaeologists concluded that its occupant – a Neanderthal hunter with a crushed skull – must have been laid to rest on a bed of brightly coloured flowers.

By the time of the Bronze Age, grave goods had become a mark of status, and the wealthy and powerful expected to depart with fortunes in copper and gold. Sometimes, in a spirit of conspicuous consumption, the treasures were cast onto funeral pyres and burned; Homer describes one such conflagration in the *Iliad*, when the hero Achilles cremates the body of his friend Patroclus.

At Egyptian funerals small figures known as *shabtis* were enclosed with the dead. These were expected to come to life in the otherworld and perform tasks on behalf of the deceased. Painted wood, tomb of Henutmehyt, Thebes, c.1295–1186BC.

A journey through or across water is common to many concepts of the afterlife, including the Greek vision of rivers encircling Hades's realm of the dead. Artist Arnold Böcklin's late 19th-century work, *Island of the Dead*, captures the dark and morbid mood which might be expected to accompany such a voyage.

which the soul spun out into its new life – but not before drinking the Waters of Oblivion, which erased the memory of all that had gone before.

Similar ideas cropped up in South America, where the journey theme was well developed. In the mythology of Bolivia's Guarayu people, the soul faced a choice immediately after death. It was confronted by two paths, one wide and welcoming, the other narrow and twisting. The correct choice was the second, for only by overcoming trials and dangers could it win through to rest.

The soul then had to cross rivers, one a torrent that could be traversed only by leaping from log to log above the gaping maws of scissor-toothed palometa fish. Then it had to find its way through a land of darkness and pass between clashing rocks. A surreal touch was provided by the need to go by a speaking tree without being beguiled by the words it had to say. There were moral challenges too, such as leaving behind what the heart most longed for without experiencing regret. If it succeeded in overcoming all these hazards, the soul found itself at last in the Land of the Ancestors. Restored to health and vigour by a dip in the Pool of Eternal Youth, it could then start to live again much as it had done before.

The Cold Road to Hel

Yet maybe the most haunting of all such final treks was the Norse one. While dead warriors were carried off to bliss in Valhalla (see page 114), the rest of humankind faced a much less pleasant journey to the far north. All who suffered the despised "straw death", at rest in bed, could look forward only to a cold tramp over bad and broken roads. To help them on their way, they were provided at the funeral with a pair of "Hel shoes" stout enough to stand up to the treatment expected en route.

For at last the soul came to the grim domain of Hel, who ruled Niflheim, the land of the dead. To enter, it had to cross Giallar, a bridge suspended above the Gjoll torrent and guarded by Modgud, a skeletal figure who demanded the traveller's lifeblood as a toll. Once over, the bloodless corpses travelled on through Ironwood, a forest with metallic leaves that jangled in the winds. And so at last they came to Hel-gate, where the monstrous dog Garm lurked in the Gnipa cave. Each new arrival had to throw him a Hel-cake, provided for them at their funeral, if they were to enter in safely. Yet for those who managed to finish the journey, all there was to expect was mist, cold and darkness – and the icy attentions of Hel herself.

Facing a Final Judgement

The concept of divine judgement is as old as recorded history, dating back to ancient Egypt. In the Hall of Two Truths dead souls had to confront Osiris himself – and a terrible fate awaited those the god found wanting, their hearts devoured by the monstrous Ammut.

Although the notion of a moral judgement determining people's eternal fate is now entrenched in most major religions, it was not always so. For many early societies, the fate of the individual after death depended on much more fortuitous circumstances. The way in which the body was treated was often of paramount importance; those that were correctly laid to rest with the proper funerary rites could expect good fortune, but the unburied might haunt the Earth as the wandering dead, caught in a limbo of despair. Traces of such beliefs lingered until recently in eastern Europe, where they fed into tales of the undead and of vampires.

Other societies – typically aristocratic ones with powerful social elites – projected their own class systems into the otherworld. Here the fate of an individual after death depended less on his conduct than on his station in life, with the richest rewards reserved for the wealthy or well-connected; the rest of the population could expect at best a pale reflection of their normal worldly state. So in ancient Peru members of the Inca clan hoped to rise up to the mansions of the sun, whose doors were closed to their subject peoples, while in much of Polynesia social rank also carried over beyond the grave.

So far as is known, the first people to introduce a moral dimension were the Egyptians. This was hardly coincidental, for the idea of an eternal reward for good conduct was one that required a settled society to take root. Hunter-gatherers engaged in a day-to-day struggle for survival, or even early farmers eking out a meagre subsistence, could hardly have been expected to embrace the concept of a universal order that the idea implies.

The Egyptian notion of the judgement of the dead was fully developed by New Kingdom times in the mid-second millennium BC. Papyrus scrolls and tomb paintings spell out the beliefs of the time in some detail. After a difficult and dangerous journey into the underworld (see pages 110–111), the soul passed the Sixth Gate to find itself in the Hall of Two Truths, the Egyptian place of judgement. There Osiris sat in majesty in the presence of his divine consort Isis and her sister Nephthys. Before them the dead person had to make a statement known as the Negative Confession. In it he or she formally denied having committed forty-two separate offences, ranging from murder and adultery to gossiping and practising usury. Prudent individuals took care to prepare their defence well in advance in consultation with temple priests; scrolls including it, along with useful spells and invocations, were buried with them in the tomb.

After this declaration of innocence came the moment of truth – literally so, for paintings show the dead person's heart being weighed in the balance against the feather symbol that represented veracity. The jackal god Anubis adjusted the scales, while ibis-headed Thoth recorded the results on a scroll. Behind him crouched a terrible monster, Ammut the Devourer, ready to eat those found to have lied. But for the innocent a happy future beckoned in the Fields of Yaru, a paradise not unlike the pleasanter parts of the Nile valley.

From Egypt the idea spread outwards. Greek myth spoke of three underworld judges – Minos, Rhadamanthus and Aeacus; so did Zoroastrian tradition in Persia, with Mithra, Sraosha and Rashnu. And the idea was by no means limited to the Near and Middle East. Other, distant lands had similar notions, often coloured by the nature of the earthly societies they knew. So Chinese souls had to negotiate a bureaucratic grilling not unlike the imperial examinations that tested the ambitious on Earth. Japan, with its tradition of autocratic military rule, had a divine despot in Emma-O, the dread lord of death who would furiously condemn wrongdoers to spend eternity scorching in a vat of molten metal. And far away across the world in modern-day New Mexico, the Pueblo peoples thought that the dead passed before a spirit guardian named Tokonaka, who assigned their fates with the calm impassivity of a Hopi village elder.

The Book of the Dead produced for a royal scribe called Hunefer, c.1285BC. Anubis leads the deceased Hunefer into the underworld judgement chamber. Depicted here is the key moment in the transformation of the dead person into an *akh*, or spirit that could help its living relatives. Accused before Osiris (right) of a catalogue of sins, the deceased's denials were tested for veracity by weighing his heart – the seat of thought and consciousness – against a feather, representing truth.

113

The Worlds of The Dead

Many cultures had their own visions of Heaven and Hell – places where the deserving were rewarded beyond the grave and wrongdoers punished. But just as common was the idea of an afterlife not so very different from what had gone before in this world.

Prevailing ideologies in the present world could have a marked effect on expectations for the next. Consider Norse views of the warriors' paradise, Valhalla. This was imagined as a vast hall, set in the glade of Glaesir. The building had 540 separate doors, each broad enough to allow 800 warriors to enter abreast. Combatants killed on the battlefield were brought there by the Valkyries (see pages 16–17) to be welcomed by the god Odin for an eternity of a kind that only a Viking could have cherished.

For the fallen heroes spent their days in battle, hewing with sword and axe amid the cries of the wounded. But by evening all the injuries received during the day had magically disappeared. Restored to blooming health, the whole company gathered in the great hall to feast on choice cuts from the great boar Saehrimnir which, like them, was made whole again on a daily basis. The meat was washed down with mead, served in foaming tankards by the Valkyries. Then the dead champions would settle down in the after-dinner glow to listen to tales of their own past battles. Meanwhile, their less fortunate compatriots were condemned to the gloom of Niflheim's great hall, known as Elvidner or "Misery", where the only dish was said to be Hunger and the knife Greed.

In Maori buildings, the houseposts linked Heaven and Earth, while the ridgepole formed the place of assembly for spirits to depart for the abode of the dead. This 19th-century carving surmounted an arched doorway and symbolized the gateway to the underworld.

Divine Otherworlds

Valhalla was self-evidently a paradise for a society in which military prowess was admired. Yet other countries' heavens and hells also reflected their own prevailing world-view. Polynesia had an alarming netherworld called Po reserved for wrongdoers and those unfortunate enough to die as a result of sorcery. In one of its corners lurked a dreaded avenger called Miru, constantly on the watch with a large net. He used it to scoop up passing souls like a butterfly-hunter catching specimens, and threw them into a great oven, where they roasted. But other spirits might have the good fortune to reach Havaiki, the Place of the Ancestors, conceived of as an island or islands in the west very much like those the local inhabitants already knew.

The notion of a paradisiacal otherworld on western islands was surprisingly widespread, and not only among insular populations. The same idea cropped up in western Europe, in Celtic visions of Avalon, the Isle of Apples to which the body of King Arthur was mystically transported after his final battle. Avalon itself was in fact a relatively late addition to the Arthurian canon, but it carried within it echoes of much earlier beliefs about western Islands of the Blessed.

Confused memories of this mystic archipelago underlay the early Irish travel epics describing wondrous journeys across the ocean, such as the Voyage of Maeldun or the later one of St Brendan. Particularly relevant to the Arthurian myth was the tale of Tadg, who sailed to a distant island where hunger was unknown and the sun was always shining, even though he and his companions had left Ireland in winter. There they found three hills, each one topped by a fortress; one was white, one silver and one gold. The first two, they learned, were the homes of long-dead rulers of Ireland, while the last was reserved for kings still to come.

By one of mythology's unexplained coincidences, very similar notions of a western island otherworld turned up in ancient Greece. The belief was already there in Homer's day, at the very start of the nation's recorded history. Was the idea brought by migrant populations who also travelled on westward to the Celtic lands? Or had there already at that early time been contact between Celtic peoples and Greek mariners sailing through the Mediterranean and the Strait of Gibraltar? The idea clashes with conventional chronologies but is not entirely impossible. All that is certain is that Homer knew of these fortunate lands where "no snow falls, strong winds do not blow and there is never any rain". The poet Hesiod described them in similar terms in the eighth century BC; there Zeus's father Cronos reigned over a terrestrial paradise for dead heroes where "the bounteous earth thrice a year bears fruit sweet as honey".

Subterranean Horrors

The likelihood that the Islands of the Blessed were a foreign importation is increased by the fact that Greece had other, entirely different traditions regarding the afterlife that may well have been more ancient. The best-known early description of

A commonplace belief among the Celts was that of an island otherworld to the west. In Britain, the Islands of the Blessed and Avalon both conformed to this notion. Steep Holm Island in the Bristol Channel appears an evocative otherworld – an impression often enhanced by the area's frequent sea mists.

the underworld also comes from Homer, in his description of Odysseus's journey there to consult the prophet Tiresias. As the *Odyssey* tells the tale, he reached it by sea, sailing northward to a land of perpetual twilight. There he lingered on the confines of Hades's realm, carrying out the instructions of the sorceress Circe to attract the spirits of the dead. The job involved digging a trench and filling it with animal blood, which instantly attracted a gibbering, fleshless horde. By drinking the blood the ghosts temporarily regained a semblance of animation and the power of speech – a detail borrowed from necromancers in Homer's day who claimed to use such practices to call up revenants.

The insights the reanimated spirits offered into this early Greek afterlife made it seem a miserable place indeed. The fleshless shades still bore the marks of the injuries or diseases that had killed them. The life they led there was so unappealing that one of their number, the hero Achilles, insisted to Odysseus that he would rather be the meanest peasant on Earth than ruler of the entire underground realm.

In fact classical views of the underworld evolved with time. Later Greek and Roman writers painted a picture of a more complex world into which the idea of rewards and punishments had at some stage been introduced. For the good dead, an eternity of joy now awaited in the Elysian Fields, which shared many features of the Islands of the Blessed; there souls enjoyed endless music and revels.

The fate of wrongdoers was very different. They were driven to Tartarus across a river of fire by the snake-haired Furies. All kinds of horrors were reserved for its inmates. There Tantalus stretched eternally for food he could never quite reach; Ixion revolved in agony on a wheel of fire; and Sisyphus was condemned to push a boulder up a hill without ever reaching the top.

The Wheel of Life being turned by Yama, the Tibetan Lord of Death. At the centre are the three cardinal faults of greed, hatred and delusion, symbolized by the pig, snake and cock. At the bottom, in the fourth of six spheres of life, is the kingdom of the hells. In most Eastern mythologies the multiple realms of hell form temporary stations in the continuous cycle of death and rebirth. In this world-view all existence is transitory. Temple *thangka* or wall hanging, 19th century.

Maybe such a bi-polar view of the afterlife comes naturally to humankind, along with the allied concepts of right and wrong or reward and punishment. Certainly it crops up in regions that could in no way have influenced one another. In that respect, the Greek Hades bears comparison with the views of a totally different culture from the opposite side of the world: that of the Hopi Indian peoples of the southwestern United States.

The Hopi place their paradise in the San Francisco Peaks north of Flagstaff, Arizona. As with Mount Olympus, the mountains are the home of gods – in the Hopi's case the *kachinas*, benevolent spirits that can manifest themselves in natural forces, in rituals in which dancers embody them, or in doll effigies. The land of the *kachinas* is a place of plenty – rich in foodstuffs and, despite the prevailing aridity, whole lakes of fresh water.

But the Hopi also have their vision of hell. They call it the Country of the Two Hearts, evil witches who mingle with the living. After death, wrongdoers are taken by the Two Hearts to their desert home and are left to fend for themselves. Walking until they can only crawl, they cry out for water, but they receive none; they beg for help, but none comes. There is only heat, dust and sun. Such people had made a wasteland of their own lives, and now it has come to reclaim them.

The Food of the Underworld

The belief that humans who ate the food of the underworld could never leave again was common to cultures all around the world.

Stories involving a taboo against eating underworld food go back to the very beginnings of recorded myth. An Akkadian story from Mesopotamia dating back to the third millennium BC describes how the god Nergal, who eventually became the ruler of the underworld, was warned on his first visit there to eat nothing or risk being trapped forever. In a Babylonian variant, the hero Adapa steadfastly refused to eat anything offered to him by the gods, only to find out later that he had been tricked; what he was actually being offered was the bread and water of life, and by turning it down he had lost the chance of immortality.

From the Middle East the motif travelled to classical Greece, where it featured memorably in the tale of Persephone (see page 59), condemned to spend part of each year in the underworld for having eaten a pomegranate seed when abducted by Hades. Celtic legend told the tale of Conle, bound forever to the otherworld after he ate an apple tossed to him by a fairy maiden. In the *Kalevala*, the hero Vainamoinen was forewarned and took care to avoid drinking the foaming tankard of beer offered him on his visit to Tuonela, the Finnish land of the dead.

Persephone (holding a garland of corn) was condemned by Zeus to spend half of each year in the underworld with her husband, Hades, after she ate the food of the dead. Greek vase, mid-4th century.

Living Visitors to the Dread Domain

Tales of journeys by the living to the land of the dead formed one of mythology's richest seams. Sometimes the visits were unintended, but more often they took the form of quests – for a dead lover, perhaps, or else to acquire secret knowledge.

One of Scotland's best-known border ballads tells of Thomas of Erceldoune, a thirteenth-century poet who encountered the Queen of Elfland on the Eildon Hills. She took him to her domain, where he stayed for seven years, remaining silent all that time on pain of never being able to return to his own country. When the term was up, the queen let him depart, giving him an apple whose flesh gave him the gift of prophecy. Returning to Erceldoune – today Earlston, in Lauderdale – he won a reputation as a seer. He lived for many years, until one evening he received word that a white doe had appeared outside his home. Recognizing it as a messenger from Elfland, he went out to follow it and was never seen again among the living.

In the story, Elfland is a Scottish version of the Celtic otherworld, and the ballad stands as a classic example of a genre of tale found world-wide. This consists of accounts of voyages undertaken by humans beyond the boundaries of the human sphere. Sometimes, as in the Thomas of Erceldoune story, the goal is an alternative reality in parallel with the familiar one of everyday life. Other examples of this kind of adventure might include the psychic journeys or "soul-flights" undertaken by shamans, for example in the Arctic world to the seabed home of Sedna, the spirit of the oceans. Some might see a similarity too with the thousands of alien abductions reported in the United States and elsewhere over recent decades.

In myth, though, the destination is most often specified as the land of the dead. Usually such an expedition is a task for heroes, but there are tales of individuals who got there almost accidentally.

One such comes from the Bantu region of Central Africa and tells of a girl called Marwe, deputized to keep monkeys off her parents' bean-field. But she let herself be distracted and the beans were stripped clean. In terror of her parents' anger, she ran to a nearby pool and threw herself in.

Now the pool was an entrance to the Land of Ghosts, where the spirits of dead ancestors lived. So at its bottom Marwe found a tunnel and a gate leading to a strange, twilight world. There she met a spirit woman who agreed to put her up in her hut in return for help with the household chores; but although Marwe did the cooking, she took care never to eat any food, for she knew that doing so would bind her irrevocably to her new and unfamiliar home (see box, page 117).

After a time she grew homesick and asked to be allowed to return to the human world. Before she could go, she was given the choice of plunging her hands into near-boiling or near-freezing water, and chose the latter. It was a wise decision, for when she withdrew her arms she found them heavy with gold bracelets adorned with precious stones. She was thus able to return to her village a wealthy woman and to marry the man of her

Hamatsa mask depicting a raven attendant of the feared Cannibal-at-the-North-End-of-the-World. It was worn in a Kwakiutl winter ceremonial associated with confronting death, during which an initiate visited the fearsome creature, which craved human flesh, was possessed by it, and was thereby able to demonstrate that he could calm it and restore normality. Native American, late 19th century.

Cheating Death

***A tale from Ghana describes how the Ashanti
trickster Dubiaku set out to cheat Death herself.***

A poor woman had eleven children and not
enough money to feed them all. So one day she
begged the Sky-Spirit to ask Death to come and
take some of them. Sky-Spirit agreed, but decided
instead to send the boys to Death. So the deity
went to where the boys were playing and dared
them – to go to Death's house, and to prove they
had been there by obtaining four objects: a pipe,
a snuff-box, a chewing-stick and a whetstone.

The boys ran off at once and were hospitably
received by Death, who fed them and put down
sleeping-mats for them next to those of her own
children. Secretly, her intention was to wait until
they were asleep and then eat them. Replete from
a good meal, ten of them were soon stretched out
and snoring. But Dubiaku remained obstinately
awake, thwarting her intentions.

Hoping to soothe him into slumber, she asked
him if there was anything she could fetch. So he
asked for a pipe of tobacco. No sooner had she
brought it than he called for a pinch of snuff. He
then requested a chewing-stick.

Death's irritation was mounting, but she could
not harm Dubiaku without risking waking the
others. So when he made his next demand – for
something to eat – she decided to indulge him one
more time, going outside to prepare some broth.
As she lit the fire, splinters from her whetstone
showered into the hut. Dubiaku picked them up
and then, with Death out of the way and the spoils
all in hand, woke up his brothers. Silently they
crept out of the back of the hut, leaving their
clothes bundled up to resemble sleeping children.

In time the broth was ready, and Death came
back in. Seeing everything so still, she decided
that Dubiaku must finally have fallen asleep. Free
at last to carry out her plan, she started to gobble
up the children – only, because the visitors had
gone, she ended up eating her own. Meanwhile
the cunning Dubiaku led his brothers back
through the bush to the safety of their own village.

choice, despite the fact that he suffered from a disfiguring skin disease – though, in the magical way of folktales, all his deformities later cleared up and he became the handsomest man in the district.

Romance is central to another group of underworld-voyager tales that could be called the Orpheus-type after the single best-known example. This is the celebrated classical myth of the musician who travelled to Hades's dark domain in search of his dead wife Eurydice, and for the beauty of his playing was permitted to take her back with him to the living world. But there was a proviso – that he must not look back at her before they had left the underworld behind them. In a moment of thoughtlessness he broke his promise, and so lost his beloved for ever.

This theme too turns out to have universal applications, cropping up in far-flung regions. From Hawaii, for instance, comes the tale of Hiku, the son of the moon goddess, and his love for the beautiful Queen Kawelu. He too descended to the underworld to find her after her premature death, though in his case he sought to achieve his ends by deception. Coating himself with an oil that

smelt of putrefaction, he lowered himself on a convolvulus stem into the abyss. The scent of the oil fooled the dark land's ruler into thinking that Hiku was simply another corpse, so enabling him to track down his lost love, whose spirit had taken the form of a butterfly. Catching it in a coconut shell, Hiku made his way back to the human world, where the queen's body still lay. There this version of the plot has a happy ending. Hiku was able to reintroduce the spirit into the body, restoring it to life. Then, to his delight, he saw Kawelu awake as if from a deep sleep, fully restored to health but with no memory of the extraordinary events that had occurred in the interim.

Another class of underworld journey is the fully fledged hero quest, a specialized sub-type of the epic trials of strength and courage described in Chapter 3 (see pages 78–103). In these cases the hero will most often undertake the dread journey in pursuit of some hidden knowledge. This was the case with the earliest of all such questers, the Sumerian Gilgamesh, who ventured beyond the ends of the Earth in a fruitless mission to win the secret of immortality. Similarly, the Norse god Odin hung on the World Tree over Niflheim for nine days, in a successful bid to obtain cognizance of runes, the keys to wisdom.

It was also a search for enlightenment that led Odysseus to make his journey to Hades's realm (see page 116). His goal was to consult Tiresias, believing the dead seer could use his prophetic powers to help him find his way home to Ithaca. In Virgil's Roman classic, the *Aeneid*, Aeneas undertook a similar expedition to find his dead father. His main motive was filial piety; yet when he finally encountered the dead man's shade, it was to hear an outline not just of his own future but also of that of the nascent Roman republic.

Yet other heroes' visits had less high-minded objectives. Mythology has its lighter side, and sometimes the dread mission was treated light-heartedly, or even played for laughs. Theseus and his friend Peirithous, in one Greek fable, invaded Hades's domain with no nobler motive than the desire to seduce the dark god's wife, Persephone.

Caves resonate with underworld associations, and in mythology they are often either abodes of the dead or places of emergence. An array of passages, as at Cox's Cave in Somerset seen here, is reminiscent of the classical Labyrinth, a complex network designed to confuse the unwary. In Greek myth, this was built by King Minos of Crete to house the Minotaur, the monstrous result of an unnatural liaison between his wife and a bull. In the medieval period, England's King Henry II was said to have built an artificial labyrinth to protect Fair Rosamond, his mistress.

A figure representing the maize god, One Hunahpu, dances out of the underworld after being released through the action of his sons, the Hero Twins, in defeating the Xibalbans. One Hunahpu carries a creature on his back that represents the three-layered cosmos: a monster's head at the bottom stands for the underworld, a woven mat at the back is the earthly realm, and the roof is a skyband with a bird for the celestial level. Painted vase, 8th century, from a noble's tomb at Buenavista, Belize.

For his pains Peirithous was condemned to spend all eternity there, though Theseus had the good fortune to be rescued by Herakles, who happened to be passing by on the way to completing the last of his twelve tasks.

The Lords of Xibalba

Yet for sheer, unalloyed insolence in face of death's dominion, there is no one in world mythology to compete with Hunahpu and Xbalanque, the Hero Twins of the *Popol Vuh*. This text, preserved in a version transcribed sometime after the Spanish Conquest of the Americas, recounts the adventures of these two semi-divine Mayan culture-heroes with relish. And the greatest of these was their encounter with the lords of Xibalba ("Place of Fright"), the Mayan land of the dead. Their motivation was revenge, for their father and uncle had been killed there in humiliating circumstances.

The tale of their exploits in Xibalba is a classic trickster account of insurmountable odds overcome and insuperable forces outwitted by ingenuity. Confronted with graven images dressed up to resemble the lords of Xibalba, they sent a mosquito to bite the real ones, making them cry out and thus reveal their hiding-places. Given lighted torches and cigars to return the following morning "just as they look now", they used red macaw feathers and fireflies to simulate the glow of the flames. And, at the climax of the story, they presented themselves before their enemies in the guise of wandering magic-workers whose powers included that of bringing the dead back to life. They exhibited their skills first on a dog and then on a person – and it was not long before the Xibalban lords themselves were volunteering for similar treatment. Needless to say, they were not revived as the others had been, and the resourceful twins' triumph was finally complete.

121

Returning to the Land of the Living

The general acceptance of a life beyond death raised a problem for those whom the "grim reaper" left behind. What if the dead chose to return, leaving the peace of the grave or the sanctuary of the otherworld to wander restlessly in the land of the living?

The Caribbean folk religion of *vodoun* or voodoo was particularly concerned with the spirits of the dead. A deceased's soul or corpse, brought back from the grave with the power to walk and talk, was known as a zombie. Sorcerers could recall the souls, as well as transform themselves into spirit animals. *Participants in Demonic Guise* by Rigaud Benoit, Haiti, 20th century.

The notion of restless spirits was widespread in the world's mythologies, and was also very ancient. Some scholars have even suggested that funeral rites initially developed as a ritual means of keeping the dead where they belonged, with the ceremonies serving as a marker separating the states of being and nothingness. For many traditions had a less clear-cut view of the point of death than the one now accepted, holding that consciousness did not necessarily end with a person's last breath. Cultures as different as those of North America's Eastern Woodlands and Zoroastrian Persia believed that the soul remained aware and continued to linger by the body for a specified time. Curiously, for both the period was the same – four days.

Usually people imagined the soul as an ethereal presence. Yet emphases differed. In pagan Scandinavia there was a belief that the bodies of the deceased experienced something not very different from their old physical existence in the grave. If they rose from it, they became the "walking dead" of northern legend – fearsome ghouls of the type that feature in the Icelandic sagas, with murder on their mind and the strength to take on even the most powerful human assailants.

The ancient Egyptians had sophisticated notions of the condition of the spirit after death that may have developed out of the melding of different local traditions. They distinguished three separate entities – the *ka*, the *ba* and the *akh*. The *ka* was a spiritual replica of the deceased that stayed in the tomb, where it required sustenance – hence the elaborate furnishing of these posthumous homes with foodstuffs and grave goods. The *ba*, in contrast, could travel freely, visiting the human world or that of the gods with equal ease; it was usually pictured in the form of a bird.

The *akh* represented the unification of the two other entities – an eagerly desired apotheosis that was a necessary precondition for eternal life.

In most cultures the spirits of the dead usually stayed close to home, lingering by the corpse after death or near the grave following burial; for that reason, cemeteries were almost always unpropitious or frightening places. They also tended to haunt familiar spots, particularly their old homes. In some traditions, including the Inca lands with their household mummies and ancient Rome with its *lares* (see pages 70–73), they were made welcome there. But other cultures took the opposite tack. Fearing such revenants, the Maori of New Zealand sometimes burned down the building where a death had occurred to discourage return visits. Special shelters for the dying were built to accommodate the custom.

Many cultures made a distinction between the friendly, or at least peaceful, dead, who had successfully made the transition to the otherworld, and restless spirits who continued to walk the Earth. The most common reason given for their sad fate was either that they had died violently or prematurely, in which case they might have to linger for the residue of their allotted time-span, or that the correct funeral rites had for some reason been neglected. Such was the case with the malign *bhuta* of India, who haunted abandoned or deserted spots and also frequented trees and

Appointment in Samarra

A celebrated Middle Eastern folktale set in the Baghdad marketplace succinctly expresses the theme of the inevitability of death when it is fore-ordained.

A servant on errands for his master was shocked to come across Death in the marketplace. But his surprise turned to terror when the grim figure raised its eyes and fixed them penetratingly on him.

Convinced that Death had come for him, he ran as fast as he could back to the house, where he at once started gathering together his few possessions. When his master found him, he had packed and was about to leave. Asked to explain himself, he stammered out the story of his sinister encounter in the bazaar. He had to get away at once, he said; he would take the desert road to the city of Samarra.

Shocked to lose a valued assistant, the master came to a bold decision. He would seek out Death and demand to know why he had scared his servant. So he went in his turn to the marketplace, and there he too saw the terrible stranger. But when he put his question, Death looked puzzled.

"Scare him?" he replied slowly. "No – surely not. But I confess that I was surprised to see him in Baghdad. You see, I have an appointment with him tomorrow. In Samarra."

123

the roofs of houses. They could never rest, but were condemned to hover constantly, casting no shadow. At night they would swoop down on sleeping people or animals, dropping diseases into their ears like venom. Their Chinese equivalent were the *gui*, who roamed the world causing misfortune and death. Particularly to be feared were the *gui* of suicide victims, who would try to tempt living victims to share their fate. Householders took elaborate precautions to keep *gui* out of their homes, even constructing small shrines or "spirit walls" to repel or at the very least placate them.

Another class of restless dead were the zombies of Africa and the Caribbean – corpses brought back to life by the spells of sorcerers. With no will of their own, they became the slaves of their psychic masters, and would do their bidding without demur. There was a parallel European tradition in the concept of necromancy – divination by communication with the dead. One much feared class of necromancer claimed to obtain knowledge of the future by reanimating dead bodies.

More rarely, the deceased could be resuscitated for benign purposes. From Hawaii came the story of a shaman called Eleio who, seeing a beautiful maiden one day, followed her to a cliff-top burial ground, where she revealed that she was the spirit of a girl who had recently passed away. After telling her parents what he had seen, Eleio entered a trance in which he was able to re-establish contact with her spirit and draw it towards him. Finally he succeeded in reuniting it with the girl's dead body by pushing it through the soles of her feet, at which point the girl revived. Subsequently she and Eleio married.

There were also many stories worldwide about ghosts that came back to the living world with a specific purpose to fulfil. Usually their mission was to settle unfinished business, often of a purely personal kind. Native North American tales of the Fatal Swing, for example, recounted how a young bride drowned while swinging out over water, only to fall into the care of a benign water spirit who regularly returned her to the lake's edge so she could continue to suckle her young baby.

In other tales, ghosts came back with a message of wider significance for the community as a whole. A strange Aztec legend from the Spanish Conquest era told how Princess Papan, a sister of the last emperor Motecuhzoma, rose from the grave the day after her funeral to warn her brother unavailingly of the approach of an armada of ships bearing an army of helmeted, grey-eyed men.

Others rematerialized seemingly with no better purpose than to batten off the living. These were the undead of the horror tradition, and they inspired terror in past times just as they do in films and stories today. The Slav world contributed not just the vampire but also the *kikimora*, the soul of an unbaptized girl who would smother people while they slept, and the *rusalka*, a mermaid-like siren who would tempt men into waters to drown. The Japanese *gaki* were spirits condemned to wander for a given time while they awaited rebirth. Part of their punishment was to suffer hunger and thirst without being able to satisfy their appetites, for they had no digestive organs. They could ease the pangs only by entering human victims, either via the bodily orifices or through sores or insect bites, and stealing their nourishment. As the *gaki* grew fatter, their hosts visibly wasted away. The only method of getting rid of the intruders was to take medicine they found unpalatable, and thereby force them out in search of fresh victims.

Many and varied were the miseries that the undead could inflict on the living. Small wonder, then, that people bedecked themselves with talismans to scare them away. But the best protection lay in placating the dead, firstly by laying them to rest in the correct manner, and then by never neglecting the posthumous courtesies and offerings that custom dictated. Tombs, funeral monuments and shrines, cemetery visits, Days of the Dead – all served their purpose in keeping the spirits in their place, which usually meant as far as possible from the land of the living.

Ghosts in Japan took an assortment of forms, some ghoulish, but others almost normal in appearance. *The Ghost of Genji's Lover, Yugao*, woodblock print by Tsukioka Yoshitoshi, 1886.

ACTS OF SACRIFICE

Known from the earliest times, sacrificial rites were originally intended as the ultimate celebration of life. Meant to reconfirm humankind's place in the cosmic order, they aimed to enhance the relationship of power between the earthly and the sacred, in some cultures in order to benefit society as a whole, in others only an elite of nobles or priests. In many areas sacrifice began because people believed the earth, gods or celestial objects needed nourishment to survive. The practice also drew on myths about the death of a primordial being, such as Pan Gu, from whose bodily remains the world was established, or an essential crop arose (see pages 22–24). Thus new life was derived from a voluntary act of creative violence. This selfless gift was remembered and re-enacted in ceremonies which inextricably linked life, death and renewal, with the rituals of the cultures of Mesoamerica among the most highly developed of all.

Left: The exact meaning of the figures found in tombs and foundations at Djenne, Mali, is a mystery. It is known that human sacrifice was practised in West Africa at the time as thanks for victory in war (when prisoners were ritually killed), as part of chiefly burial rites and as a form of ancestral worship. This 13th-century terracotta horseman – whose red colouring was associated with death – probably represents a symbolic offering from the post-sacrifice era.

Above: Kali, the cult name of Durga, the Indian goddess of death and destruction. Often depicted smeared with blood, fanged and wearing a necklace of skulls and earrings of corpses, she was a fearsome sight to behold. Until the 19th century, her devotees practised *thuggee*, bloodlessly garroting male victims as sacrificial offerings to her.

Left: In Shang China the souls of deceased ancestors were sustained by sacrifices. When a dead ruler was buried, animals and humans were often killed in the vast royal tombs in rituals similar to those found in Africa. Although the practice was abandoned early on, the cult of royal ancestor worship remained, alongside a belief in the emperor as a divine founder-father of the people. Bronze decapitating axe, Shang era (1766–1027BC).

Above: Blood was often considered the sacred life-force, used by the gods in some myths to create humankind. Central America's Maya nobility practised auto-sacrifice to nourish the earth, thank the gods, renew ancestral links and bolster their earthly power. This lintel glyph, one of a series from Yaxchilan, Chiapas, AD726, shows a princess receiving a vision following the burning of paper soaked in blood dripped from her pierced tongue.

Elsewhere in the Americas, ritual killing and bloodshed were practised quite widely. Mexico's Aztecs built an important mountain-top shrine dedicated to the rain god, Tlaloc, and a child was sacrificed on the peak each spring, the blood being used to bathe a statue of the deity in the hope of averting drought. In similar vein, the Inca people of Peru slaughtered animals and even adolescent children as offerings to their mountain gods.

AN ENDURING LEGACY

Mythology is a modern notion. Built into the very nature of the word is the idea that the stories that make it up are not true. Yet such a view would have seemed bizarre, if not sacreligious, to the people who originally told them, for whom they served in lieu of science and history as an explanation of the universe and of people's place in it. By the time they came to be categorized as myth, these mind-shaping narratives were inevitably diminished.

What changed the situation was, first, the coming of the great religions, and then the scientific revolution. The very success of Christianity, Islam and Buddhism was in a way a commentary on the limitations of the older beliefs, which usually lacked the prescriptions for personal salvation that gave the new faiths their profound appeal. In contrast, mythology's gods were mighty manifestations of nature's powers, and they had little to provide in terms of loving care or compassion. Although there were pockets of resistance, the old beliefs were, on the whole, abandoned without a struggle.

Below: Few buildings better exude the spirit of times past than ruined castles, firing the imagination of successive generations. Lackeen Castle in County Tipperary, Ireland.

Then, from the seventeenth century onwards, science came along to deride ideas about the workings of the world that the myths had fostered. With the spread of new, experimentally verified knowledge, mythology lost its last shreds of credibility as a system for explaining the universe. Its most cherished notions now came to seem the height of naivety, at best childish fairytales, at worst deliberate attempts to deceive.

And yet, surprisingly, the stories survived. Even at the height of eighteenth-century rationalism, educated people all over the Western world still immersed themselves in the classical myths. With the coming of the Romantic movement at the end of the century, new interest also developed in the old Norse and Celtic tales. Soon folklorists were combing the world beyond Europe to save whatever was left of the heritage of story.

And in time the modern world produced myths of its own. These were very different from what had gone before, yet they drew on the great narratives of the past for some of their inspiration and much of their imaginative power. In the cinema and video, they found media uniquely suited for making fantasies real and giving the marvellous the sheen of veracity. And even the old route of oral transmission still played a part, spreading urban legends that in their own way echoed ancient tradition, by embodying secret hopes and fears.

Opposite: Countless ancient rituals survive into the present. Burning out the old year still occurs in parts of Britain. At Allendale in Northumberland, costumed men carry blazing barrels of tar on their heads in a custom aimed at driving out evil for the coming year.

The Twilight of the Gods

In time the great religions supplanted the myths. But the old beliefs rarely died out totally; instead they went underground, often to resurface in the form of legend or folklore.

In part, the fate of the myths depended on the attitude adopted by the faith that took their place. Buddhism, for instance, was generally tolerant towards the old stories, happily accepting them into its broad embrace. In Tibet, for example, the old Bon religion in time became inextricably woven into the fabric of the new belief. Indian Hinduism and Japanese Shintoism went even further, being in large part based on the nations' ancestral beliefs. There, priests added an organizational framework and a structure of worship, but in other respects did little to disrupt the continuum of past tradition.

Christianity and Islam, however, were both deeply antagonistic to the old, pagan gods. Muslims in theory tolerated the views of non-believers in the countries they conquered, though in practice they took steps to discourage them.

So adherents of the ancient Zoroastrian creed in Persia were officially permitted to practice their religion, but in reality discrimination ensured that most people converted to the new faith.

Christianity was even less prepared to put up with the belief-systems it supplanted. First in Europe, then later in other parts of the world, it imposed its will by peaceful evangelization where possible, but by the threat of violence if that provided insufficient inducement. The combination proved highly effective – so much so that in Europe most visible traces of the old pagan religions of the Celtic west and the Slavic east were wiped out. So, later, were the pre-Columbian rites of the New World.

Yet even in those lands, something survived. Beliefs and customs that could not express themselves openly went underground, infusing the local forms of Christianity with a distinctive flavour of their own. In the Slav lands the fusion became known as the Dual Faith, and its influence lingered well into the twentieth century. And in South America too, Roman Catholicism took on an

In many parts of the world the major religions coexist with enduring indigenous beliefs. In South America, for example, strong elements of native culture have been retained. These Indian elders in the Andes are attending a meeting in church.

The Little People

Like the fairies of Ireland, elves, dwarfs and gnomes all trace their origins deep into the mythological past.

The original home of the little people of mythology was Alfheim, one of the nine realms of Norse cosmology. Initially they bred like maggots in the flesh of Ymir, the primordial giant. The gods in time divided them into two groups, based on appearance and temperament. The Dark Elves, whose nature was secretive and earthy, were sent to live as miners underground, where they became the progenitors of the dwarfs, gnomes and goblins of northern folklore. The Light Elves inherited airy Alfheim proper, situated between Heaven and Earth. Their descendants were the elves and fairies.

In the way of folk traditions, other elements complicated this straightforward division as the centuries passed. Thus the gnomes took their characteristics from the Scandinavian dwarfs, but the name itself came from the word *gnomus* coined by the German-Swiss alchemist Paracelsus. In his schema, they were the elemental spirits associated with the earth.

Other contributors were Clotho, Lachesis and Atropos, the Three Fates who in classical mythology allotted each new-born child its destiny and lifespan. In time they became the *fees* of French and the *fata* of Italian legend, who in medieval

tradition visited houses where a baby had been born bearing gifts of good or bad fortune. As such, they were the ancestors of all the fairy godmothers of later story.

Fairies dancing happily in a circle beneath the trees. Illustration by Florence Harrison from *Elfin Song*.

individual identity; the Church calendar in time found room for Christian adaptations of traditional festivals, and popular saints took on some of the attributes of the old pagan gods.

Another route by which the old beliefs could leave a trace was through folklore and legend. The divinities of pagan times vanished, but only to reappear as nature sprites haunting the countryside where they had once been worshipped. In the process, they were often physically diminished. So the Tuatha de Danaan, the children of the goddess Dana who in legendary times ruled all Ireland, literally shrank to become the fairies and little people of rural tradition. In the popular imagination, their homes were the mounds or barrows in which the real-life rulers of the land had long ago been laid to rest.

Further indignities awaited. In the eighteenth and nineteenth centuries, urban sophisticates who rejected the superstitions of the countryside out of hand nonetheless fell in love with the charm of the old beliefs and the stories that accompanied them. They found a new role for these, bowdlerized and sentimentalized, as entertainments for children; and so the fairytale was born. An even unlikelier fate awaited the Dark Elves of Norse myth (see box, above). Robbed of their sinister aspect as malign earth spirits, they found new incarnations as decorative garden gnomes.

Yet something has survived all the changes. The best fairytales still retain the power to fire the imagination and inspire awe; and as knowledge of past beliefs is painstakingly resurrected, an awareness of the veneration they once inspired resurfaces too. The old gods may be gone for good; yet even so, something of their numinous presence still haunts the woods and hills where in ancient times they were revered.

An Unquenched Thirst for Legend

Although mythology's role as a way of understanding the world may have faded, people still need myths to live by. In particular, the demand for heroes is as strong as it ever was.

If the great religions weakened mythology's grip as a belief-system, the scientific revolution sounded its death-knell. In the light of the savants' relentless probing, the traditional explanations the myths provided came to seem lame indeed. Many of the wilder theories that the creative imagination, untrammelled by facts, had devised to explain the universe were shown to be just that. There was no gigantic turtle supporting the world, as the ancient Chinese and some Native American peoples had believed. The rain now fell as a result of the hydrological cycle, not because the god Tlaloc chose to send it, for all that the Aztecs and other Mesoamerican peoples had claimed. The stars were distant suns, not the souls of dead pharaohs in the way ancient Egyptians had maintained, or holes in the floor of Heaven as certain Arctic peoples would have had it.

By dispassionately investigating the universe and its physical mechanisms, science quite literally exploded many myths. It produced alternative hypotheses to explain the world's workings that were in every respect more convincing than the wild surmisings they replaced. Yet, even so, something about the scientists' deadpan objectivity rendered their own world-view less than totally satisfactory. Science was shaped rigorously to the demands of human reason; but mythology had been cast in the mould of the imagination and the emotions, and for them the new analytical outlook had little place.

In practice that meant that some parts of mythology's traditional role had been upstaged, but not others. Only in the most remote and back-ward areas of the world did people still look to the myths for an explanation of the mechanics of the cosmos. And even on the biggest questions of the meaning and purpose of life and the significance of death, for which science had no convincing answers, most people turned to religion rather than to myth to find solutions. But that still left one area where the old traditions had not been

A Chinese Communist propaganda poster from 1950 shows the masses in Beijing's Tiananmen Square acclaiming ideological heroes of the revolution, including Lenin, Stalin and Chairman Mao. The men's elevated status was not unlike that of the divine emperor in former times.

The creation of *Star Wars* by George Lucas was a conscious attempt to develop a "film cycle" deriving many of its undercurrents from popular mythology. Its immense global success is testament to the enduring appeal of such basic themes as the struggle between good and evil, fate and chance, order and chaos, heroic will and divine force. Alec Guinness plays Jedi Knight Ben Kenobi, in *Star Wars: Special Edition*, released in 1997 for the first film's tenth anniversary.

supplanted. Nothing had replaced the hero tale, and yet people's need for human exemplars of strength, courage and resolution remained as strong as ever.

One result has been a lingering fascination with the traditional champions of legend. Across much of the world Herakles and Odysseus are still household names. More locally, Chinese-speakers still thrill to the exploits of Guan Yu and Nezha, Japanese to those of Yorimitsu and Yoshitsune, English-speakers to Robin Hood and King Arthur, Central Americans to the feats of the Hero Twins, Indians to the epic protagonists of the *Ramayana* and *Mahabharata* and Iranians to Rustam, Isfandiyar and other warriors of the *Shahnameh*.

Yet at least since the Romantic era at the start of the nineteenth century, people have also felt a need for new heroes reflecting the changing nature of the modern world. At first they looked mostly to real-life figures: Lord Byron, Garibaldi, Victor Hugo – or, on a less exalted plane, to Ned Kelly and Wyatt Earp. But with the development of the mass media in the twentieth century, a whole new world of possibilities opened.

Sinisterly enough, politicians in totalitarian states were among the first to explore the media's potential. The Bolshevik leader Lenin was one of the first to appreciate their promise as channels for propaganda. Although he eschewed using them to develop a cult of personality, his successor Stalin had no such qualms. Mussolini, Hitler and Chairman Mao all similarly employed film and print to build up carefully stage-managed images as more-than-human figures of faultless strength and wisdom – a perversion of the true heroic spirit that nonetheless proved alarmingly successful.

One reason why was the birth of cinema, whose need for strong storylines and central characters with whom the viewer could identify fed the demand tirelessly. In a sense, the entire Hollywood star system as it developed in the 1920s and 1930s served that purpose. Blown up much larger than life on the silver screen and watched in a darkness that resembled that of sleep and dreams, actors and actresses took on the glamour of the parts they played and some ended up acquiring a mythic dimension. Studio biographies liked to stress such elements of the classic hero-myth life-pattern as a difficult early childhood (see pages 86–91). Death played a part too; the early demise of such figures as Rudolf Valentino and James Dean took on a real aura of

133

legend, just as those of the rock stars Jimi Hendrix, Janis Joplin Jim Morrison, Elvis Presley and Kurt Cobain would do in later days.

Cinema also needed fictional heroes for the stars to play, and one rich source of inspiration turned out to be the lowly comic-strip. Flash Gordon, Batman and Superman (see box, below) all made the transfer to the big screen, as did Fantomas in France. Other exemplars came from books. The super-spy James Bond, an Achilles of the early technological era, was the unlikely creation of the foreign manager of London's *Sunday Times* newspaper, the Old Etonian Ian Fleming.

The cinema also inherited another function that in earlier times had been the task of mythology: that of confronting and expressing people's

primal fears. Some of the most hair-raising figures of legend – vampires, werewolves, zombies – made a direct transition to the movies, which gave them much more widespread exposure than they had ever had before. The monsters that had always haunted the mythic imagination also soon had their equivalents on celluloid, and a whole special-effects (SFX) cottage industry grew up in Los Angeles to flesh out nightmare visions in papier-mache and wire. In time new creations took their place in the bestiary of the imagination: King Kong and Godzilla rivalled Polyphemus, Antaeus and the other giants of classical legend; the Creature from the Black Lagoon stood in for Beowulf's Grendel; snake-haired Medusa found an echo in the Bride of Frankenstein's electric-shock coiffure.

The Birth of Superman

Of all the modern-day fictional heroes, Superman still stands supreme – and he was deliberately modelled by his creator, writer Jerry Siegel, on the strong men of classical myth, becoming a one-man blend of Herakles, Samson and other enduring figures of legend.

The Man of Steel made his first appearance in the pages of Action Comics in 1938. He was created by writer Jerry Siegel, who probably borrowed the name from George Bernard Shaw's play, *Man and Superman*. Shaw himself had coined the term as a translation of the German philosopher Friedrich Nietzsche's *ubermensch*, literally "overman". The idea reflected a belief that ordinary man had it within him to release untold potential.

In the 1930s, Nietzsche's ideas were being exploited by the Nazis in Germany, as Siegel was well aware. He first used the term at high school in a story called "The Reign of the Superman" about a mad scientist-type dictator. But some time later he had a flash of insight. As he later described the moment, he was trying to get to sleep one night when ". . . all of a sudden it hits me. . . I conceive of a character like Samson, Hercules, and all of the strong men I ever heard tell of rolled into one. Only more so." Superman was born.

Siegel also owed a considerable debt to classical mythology in amassing Superman's superhuman

powers. Here he cited the example of the Argonauts who sailed with Jason in search of the Golden Fleece. "Besides Herakles," he wrote, "there were Zetes and Malais, who flew; Euphemos, the super-speedster; Kaineus, who was invulnerable; and even Lynkeus who, we are told, could see things underground – yes, X-ray vision."

As the character evolved, many other features of the classic hero myth found their way into the storyline. Superman's birth on the dying planet Krypton and subsequent dispatch to Earth echoed the familiar abandoned-child theme of the tradition (see box, page 87). His normal suburban upbringing by Martha and Jonathan Kent, interspersed with occasional feats of highly abnormal strength, recalled that of many earlier champions of justice. But there was one savvy addition to the mythic canon – his earthbound persona as the mild-mannered reporter Clark Kent. Through this dual-identity device, Superman became Everyman, a figure with whom even the least heroic reader could identify.

J.K. Rowling's 1997 creation Harry Potter enchanted children worldwide and captured the interest of a lot of parents too. Planned as a series of seven, the novels to date have explored many themes, including supernatural powers, fantastical travel and self-discovery. Early on, bespectacled orphan Harry finds out that he is a wizard and his strange boarding school is actually Hogwarts School of Witchcraft and Wizardry. In the third adventure, *Harry Potter and the Prisoner of Azkaban*, Harry learns more about who he really is, what his potential powers are and the fact he has deadly enemies who must be thwarted. Harry is seen here riding with his friend Hermione on the back of Buckbeak, the strange "hippogriff" creature which is half bird and half horse.

Sophisticated observers tended to view the entire horror genre as tawdry and foolish, much as their counterparts in ancient Greece had treated the more sensational elements in the myths themselves. Yet there were also attempts to draw directly upon mythology for more ambitious creative ends. The fantasy movement in literature is rooted in the work of William Morris, the English poet and designer, whose *The Wood Beyond the World* and *The Well at the World's End* drew on medieval romance traditions. His most extraordinary successor was J.R.R. Tolkein, whose epic *Lord of the Rings* was recently voted the most popular novel among English-speakers. A professor of Anglo-Saxon, Tolkien was deeply versed in Nordic legend, and almost every element in his great creation can be traced back to traditional lore.

The spirit of fantasy also remained very much alive in children's literature, which in many respects kept closer to the mythological spirit of improbable adventure than its adult counterpart. In its early days folklore fed directly into it via the work of such anthropologists as Germany's Grimm brothers or Denmark's P.C. Asbjornsen and through traditional collections like the *Thousand and One Nights*. Soon, however, authors were devising their own original wonder tales and setting them in imaginary worlds. L. Frank Baum's Oz and C.S. Lewis's Narnia both contained many elements of myth; but the most successful of all such enterprises may yet turn out to be the Harry Potter books of the English author J.K. Rowling. Replete with wizards, magic, fantastic creatures and figures of evil, they quickly won themselves a world audience in the late 1990s.

Modern myth of the Tolkien or Rowling variety obviously bears only a superficial resemblance to the real thing. After all, it makes no claim to be anything other than invention, it is the product of named individuals and it sets out simply to entertain. Yet, at its best, it touches some of the same imaginative responses that gave the old stories their enduring power. In a new style and format, it nonetheless addresses the same human needs.

Folklore Enters the Space Age

Ironically, the triumph of science spawned a folklore of its own in the UFO-mania of the 1950s and 1960s. At the same time, age-old fears and phobias found new outlets in the streetwise guise of "urban legends".

There were obvious reasons why space should have exerted such a grip on the popular imagination at a time when travel beyond the confines of the Earth first became a reality and the invention of nuclear weapons made the planet seem unexpectedly fragile. The possibility of life existing elsewhere in the universe suddenly no longer appeared far-fetched. But while scientists spent millions of dollars searching for extra-terrestrial intelligence through radio telescopes, the public for the most part sated its curiosity with science-fiction and B-movies. More intriguing in many ways were the supposedly real accounts of sightings of UFOs – unidentified flying objects. There were reports, too, of even closer alien encounters, for, in one of the weirder eccentricities of the Space Age, the century during which humankind sent astronauts to the moon also experienced several thousand people worldwide claiming to have personally been the victims of alien abduction.

In some respects the UFO reports shared similarities with so-called "urban legends", which like them claimed to be true and travelled by word of mouth on the "bush telegraph" – or latterly on the internet, which provided an unparalleled platform to give local gossip global exposure.

The legends – described by Jan Harald Brunvand, a prominent collector, as "realistic stories concerning recent events (or alleged events) with an ironic or supernatural twist" – have always been particularly popular with teenagers, who pass them on at college, camps or parties. It is hardly surprising, then, that a lot of them involve young people in jeopardy, cut off temporarily from family and friends – while baby-sitting, for instance, or on a date at night. That is the setting for one of the best-known examples. "The Hook"

Recent technological advances have enabled us to assess Earth's relative insignificance in the cosmos and led many people to look beyond our galaxy for answers. Today, the mundane but longstanding anxieties addressed in myth vie with UFOs and extra-terrestrial intelligence for public interest. One focus of modern legend is the "crop circle" phenomenon, sometimes explained as the markings left in fields by visiting alien craft.

describes how a courting couple, parked in a secluded lover's lane, hear on their car radio that a killer with a hook for a hand is on the loose. Scared by a sudden noise, they speed away – only to find a hook hanging from the car door handle when they get home.

Other stories are even more evidently mythic in their implications. Perhaps the best-known of them all is the tale of the vanishing hitch-hiker. Its many variant versions all tell of a lone individual picked up by the roadside late at night who disappears in unexplained circumstances before reaching the address he or she has given. Invariably, the driver goes there the next day to try to cast light on the mystery, and always it is to learn that the person he had helped is dead – usually killed in a road accident. The enigma of death itself, the undying urge to go home again, wandering spirits trapped endlessly on the road between existence and extinction – these subjects could not be closer to the mythological tradition.

Such stories are, of course, entertaining too – and in the past this was also one of the less feted functions of mythology. In baronial halls or around camp fires, narrators recounted the old tales partly for the pleasure of mesmerizing an audience, and people listened to them to laugh or to feel sympathy, awe or fear. In so doing they were able to confront, in public, emotions that otherwise might have remained bottled up. The story-telling acted as therapy, enabling them to face up to their secret hopes and fears. So it is too in many ways with the cornucopia of urban legends. In fresh channels, the old current still flows on.

The Origins of Astrology

The roots of modern astrology can be traced back to the Middle East, through the work of the first astronomers in Mesopotamia and Egypt almost 5,000 years ago.

By about 400BC, astronomers had divided the northern-hemisphere sky into twelve equal segments, and the zodiac had been born. The work was done by Chaldean savants operating from Babylon, who assigned to each sign a symbolic significance: Libra, for instance, was already associated with balance and judgement.

The subject reached a peak of intellectual prestige in the Hellenistic world of the last two centuries BC. Scholars working in Alexandria incorporated into the Mesopotamian schema a knowledge of the decans – thirty-six bright stars, identified by ancient Egyptian astronomers, whose risings were separated by ten-day intervals. Each one was seen as the manifestation of a god who had power over the period in which it appeared.

Largely forgotten in the Dark Ages, astrology was reintroduced to medieval Europe in the twelfth century AD from Arab sources that had helped preserve the heritage of classical learning. It soon won huge popularity, despite opposition from the Church. By the later Middle Ages there were chairs of astrology at universities in Paris, Bologna and Florence.

The Copernican revolution of the sixteenth century marked the death-knell for astrology as a serious science, for its world-view no longer made sense if the Earth was not the centre of the universe but merely a planet revolving around the sun. Yet the subject has more than retained its hold on the popular imagination, with an estimated 10,000 professional astrologers at work today in the United States alone.

A detail from November in the 15th-century *Tres Riches Heures du Duc de Berry*.

Index

Page numbers in *italic* denote captions. Where there is a textual reference to the topic on the same page as a caption, italics have not been used.

Further Reading

Aldington, R. and Ames, D. (trans.) *New Larousse Encyclopedia of Mythology*, Hamlyn: London, 1968
Campbell, J *The Hero with a Thousand Faces*, Princeton University Press: Princeton, 1972
Campbell, J *The Masks of God*, Viking Press: New York, 1959–64
Courlander, H. *A Treasury of African Folklore*, Marlowe & Company: New York, 1996
Eliade, M. *Gods, Godesses and Myths of Creation*, New York, 1974
The New Encyclopedia Britannica, 15th edition, Chicago, 1991
Farmer, P. (ed.) *Beginnings: Creation Myths of the World*, Atheneum: New York, 1979
Freund, P. *Myths of Creation*, Washington Square Press: New York, 1965
Graves, R. *The Greek Myths*, Penguin: London, 1992
Hamilton, V. *In the Beginning: Creation Stories from around the World*, Harcourt Brace Jovanovich: New York, 1988
Leach, M. *The Beginning: Creation Myths around the World*, Thomas Y. Crowell: New York, 1956
Leeming, D. *The World of Myths*, Oxford University Press: Oxford, 1992
Leeming, D. and Leeming, M. *A Dictionary of Creation Myths*, Oxford University Press: Oxford, 1994
Long, C.H. *Alpha: The Myths of Creation*, George Braziller: New York, 1963
Long, C.H. "Cosmogony" in *The Encyclopaedia of Religion*, 16 vols edited by M. Eliade, Macmillan: New York, 1987
Lowry, S.P. *Familiar Mysteries: The Truth in Myth*, Oxford University Press: Oxford, 1982
Maclagan, D. *Creation Myths: Man's Introduction to the World*, Thames & Hudson: London, 1977
McLeish, K. *Myth: Myths and Legends of the World Explored*, Bloomsbury: London, 1996
Miller, M. and Taube, K. *The Gods and Symbols of Ancient Mexico and the Maya*, Thames & Hudson: London, 1993
Myth and Mankind series (20 volumes), Time-Life Books: Alexandria, Virginia, 1996–2000
O'Brian, J. and Major, W. *In the Beginning: Creation Myths from Ancient Mesopotamia, Israel, and Greece*, Scholars Press: Chico, California, 1982
Oleyar, R. *Myths of Creation and Fall*, Harper & Row: New York, 1975
Parrinder, G. *African Mythology*, Hamlyn: London, 1982
Sproul, B.C. *Primal Myths: Creation Myths around the World*, HarperCollins: San Francisco, 1991
Van Over, R. *Sun Songs: Creation Myths from around the World*, Dutton: New York, 1980

Picture Credits